Quattro Pro for Windows

David Royall

TEACH YOURSELF BOOKS

Long-renowned as the authoritative source for self-guided learning —with more than 30 million copies sold worldwide — the *Teach Yourself* series includes over 200 titles in the fields of languages, crafts, hobbies, sports, and other leisure activities.

British Library Cataloguing in Publication Data
A CIP catalogue record is available from the British Library

Library of Congress Catalog Card Number: 93-85127

First published in UK 1994 by Hodder Headline Plc, 338 Euston Road, London NW1 3BH

First published in US 1994 by NTC Publishing Group, 4255 West Touhy Avenue, Lincolnwood (Chicago), Illinois 60646 – 1975 U.S.A.

Typeset by Multiplex Techniques, Orpington, Kent.
Printed in England by Cox & Wyman Ltd, Reading, Berkshire.

Impression number	14	13	12	11	10	9	8	7	6	5	4	3	2
Year		1999		1998		1997		1996		1995		1994	

CONTENTS

1

— GETTING STARTED —

—— 1.1 Aims of this chapter ——

This chapter gives an outline of what the Quattro Pro™ spreadsheet is, what it can do and how you should prepare your computer for its use.

There is also an explanation of some computer terminology that may be new to you. It will help you get started and ensure that you have what is needed to be successful in using the Quattro Pro product.

—— 1.2 What is a spreadsheet? ——

A spreadsheet is the electronic equivalent of an accountant's ledger – a large piece of paper divided by vertical columns and horizontal rows into a grid of cells. The name derives from the spreading of the organisation's accounts on a sheet of paper and the user can directly enter numbers, formulae or text into the cells.

Screen dump 1.1 shows what an empty spreadsheet might look like.

The screen dump has been taken from Quattro Pro for Windows version 5.0 and may differ a little compared to what you will see if you have a different version.

There are letters along the columns at the top and numbers in rows down the left side of the spreadsheet working area. The section in the middle of the blank area which is outlined in black is referred to as a cell. Each cell is identified by its co-ordinates, like a map reference or point on a graph. The highlighted section here is at C5, i.e. *column* C and *row* 5.

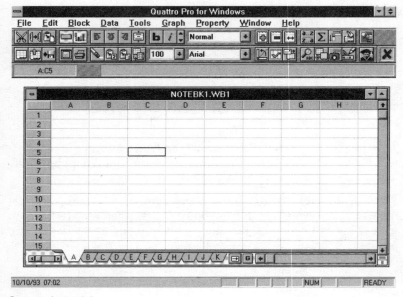

Screen dump 1.1

Use your mouse to navigate from cell to cell.

● Click on cell B1, type a number (e.g. 4) and press the Enter key.

● Click on cell C1, type another number (e.g. 6) and press the Enter key.

● Then click on A1 and type +B1*C1 and press the Enter key.

Cell A1 displays the number typed in cell B1 multiplied by the number you typed in cell C1. Type a different number in cell B1 or C1 and press the Enter key. The number displayed in cell A1 will automatically change.

Note that you need to precede a formula with + or =. The spreadsheet effectively becomes a screen based calculator capable of being printed or displayed as a graph.

As a 'tool', accountancy is by no means the only work for which spreadsheets can be used.

Some examples of the power of spreadsheets are:

1   What if? analysis

Any figure can be changed at any time and the new results will automatically be shown. Thus a 'What if?' analysis might be: What if sales were to increase by 10%? The spreadsheet can calculate this easily. This facility of being able to recalculate formulae quickly makes spreadsheets a powerful, useful and popular analytical tool.

2   Goal seeking

Some spreadsheets are used in order to seek goals. For example, spreadsheets can be set up to depict the sales and costs of a business where a model is set up to determine at what price profits will be maximised.

3   Graphing

In this instance, the spreadsheet is used to represent tables and figures in the form of graphs.

4   Storing records of information

A spreadsheet can be used to hold records of information such as details of costs accumulated for a specific job. Such information can be altered quickly and can be used as the basis of a contract tender or for price determination. This type of application is often referred to as a **database**.

In practice, spreadsheets will be used for a combination of the above. Spreadsheets are flexible modelling tools which can be readily adapted for many jobs involving repetitive numerical calculations.

Other examples of their use:

- Financial plans and budgets can be represented as a table, with columns for time periods (e.g. months) and rows for different elements of the plan (e.g. costs and revenue).

- Tax, investment and loan calculations.

- Statistics can be displayed such as averages, standard deviations, time series and regression analysis. Many in–built statistical functions are available in Quattro Pro for Windows.

- Merging branch or departmental accounts to form group (consolidated) accounts. This involves merging 2 or more spreadsheets together.

- Currency conversion; this is useful for an organisation with overseas interests.

- Timetabling and roster planning of staff within organisations or departments.

- In an educational establishment, the recording of class lists, attendance, student marks.

You will probably think of many more potential applications as you work through the book. Quattro Pro is a product developed by a company called Borland and incorporates three standard applications: spreadsheet, database, and graphics. Uses of spreadsheets often combines these three applications.

—— 1.3 Hardware and software ——

'Hardware' refers to the physical components of a computer system, while 'software' refers to the programs that are used to give instructions to the computer. Both are needed if the computer is to achieve anything at all.

Software for a computer will come in many forms; essentially there will be an operating system which will come with the computer system and applications software which you normally buy as extra. Quattro Pro for Windows is an example of applications software. For those of you who are using Quattro Pro in a Windows environment, you will also need Microsoft Windows™ software which is an extra application used with an operating system.

When the machine is switched on, the computer will need some instructions about how to operate the computer system, hence the term 'operating system'. Different computers will have varying kinds of operating systems and this needs to be considered when you are buying applications.

When choosing hardware, you will need to make decisions on such issues as how much hard disk space you will need and the quality of your printer. When selecting software, you are making decisions about what you want your computer to do for you.

—————— 1.4 Computer needs ——————

There is now a large range of computer types on the market from which you can choose. Use of the Quattro Pro package tends to be associated with a microcomputer. In other words, a computer that stands by itself and allows one person to sit at a keyboard and operate it. However, there are other types of systems such as networks and multi–user systems on which you will find Quattro Pro for Windows being used. If you are buying Quattro Pro for Windows, you must know which type of system you will be working with.

Version 5.0 of Quattro Pro for Windows has a special 'Workgroup' facility which allows users to share information between each other on a network system. This can be especially useful if you are part of a team making use of common spreadsheets or want to send a copy of a spreadsheet for someone else to view. In fact, with the correct communications hardware and software, you can distribute information contained in spreadsheets across any geographical area whether local, national or international.

—————— 1.5 Operating systems ——————

Although all computers appear similar from the outside, they may well have different operating systems. An operating system is the language that any particular machine has to work with, in much the same way that different peoples of the world communicate in different languages.

Most microcomputers use the operating system MS-DOS (Microsoft Disk Operating System). However, there are different versions of MS-DOS. The different versions have come about because computers have advanced over the years with new and more powerful devices and changes in the operating systems have been required for the new devices to be operated. As you will be working with Quattro in a Windows environment, the Windows software is additional to MS-DOS, but still needs an operating system for it to function.

Increasingly the operating system OS/2 (Operating System 2) is being used. This has the added advantage over MS-DOS that many 'jobs' can be executed at the same time. For example, while the computer is printing, an operator can get on with something else without any slowdown in speed. Alternatively, it will allow operators the facility of being able to work on a number of different packages at the same time from one machine.

Network systems require a different operating system again because there will be a number of different machines all working from a common system (normally called a file server). The network operating system will, for example, need to administer all machines using the same software package and a single printer.

With such a range of systems, it is important that before you embark on purchasing a copy of Quattro Pro you check with your supplier that the version of Quattro Pro you are purchasing matches the machine and operating system you are intending to put it on.

——— 1.6 Processor types ———

Part of the computer's hardware is called the processor. All computers need such processing devices as they form the main attributes of a computer system. Over the last few years such processors have become more sophisticated and more powerful.

Not all software packages will run on all processors; so, again, you need to be careful that the software purchased is correct for the machine you have. It is not for a book like this to discuss the varying processor types nor is it necessary for you to know all about them in order to be able to take full advantage of this Quattro package. However, you will need to know what kind of processor you have if you are going to purchase software. Most dealers will be able to identify this by the model of machine you have.

——— 1.7 Disk drives ———

Getting a computer with the correct disk drives is important. On microcomputers you normally find two types of disk drive, a floppy disk drive and a hard disk drive.

A hard disk normally comes already installed into your machine and cannot easily be removed. It is capable of holding a very large volume of data and is used by the computer when it is running the software. It will be needed to hold the software as well as the data generated by the spreadsheet.

A floppy disk drive is used to store data on removable small disks. When you receive software, it normally comes on such floppy disks. You will then need to copy the data on to the computer's hard disk – a process called installation. Clear instructions on how to carry this out will come with the software. Such drives typically require disks of one of two sizes; 3.5 inches or 5.25 inches. When buying software, you will need to advise your supplier as to what size of floppy drive you are using to install your software. Older machines may be equipped with both sizes of drive. Floppy disk drives are also needed for backing up data as a precaution against loss of data.

For both types, the amount of data that can be stored will vary from device to device. Hard disks normally store from 60 megabytes upwards, while a 3.5 inch floppy disk stores 1.44 megabytes. In practice, if you are a Windows user, you should have far more disk storage than 60 megabytes.

It is often difficult to appreciate what a megabyte of data actually is, but to give you some idea, a book of this size, if converted to computer data, would fit on to a 1 megabyte disk. When software is purchased, it will normally come on a number of floppy disks with commercial packages taking up to 28 megabytes of disk storage. Remember, apart from the software package, your computer will also have to store all the data generated by the software.

1.8 Screen types

At first sight it may seem that one screen on a computer is very much like any other. However, there are now many variations. There is first of all the straight choice of colour and monochrome. Many portable computers and notebook computers will only have a monochrome display.

All new machines will have full graphics capabilities. Older computers will vary in their ability to display graphics. Quattro Pro for Windows will require such graphics capabilities to operate.

1.9 Printers

You will almost certainly want to print out spreadsheets and graphs. Not all printers will necessarily be able to do this.

Printers will vary in speed of print, quality of print and paper width (usually 80-column or 132-column width). Also, older printers may not be capable of printing graphs.

Here is a list of the main types of printer available and briefly what they can achieve.

Dot matrix These are in common use but are being replaced by ink jet machines, for low budget users. A 24-pin printer will print with greater definition than a 9-pin printer. Dot matrix printers will also produce graphics output.

Laser printers These give the best output. They work rather like a photocopier and can produce art work for publishing. They are expensive, however, and cannot print carbon copies.

Ink jet printers These offer high quality at low cost. Colour ink jet printers are now becoming cheaper and are an attractive option.

Whatever kind of printer is purchased you will need to make sure that Quattro Pro for Windows is able to send data to that printer for printing. In practice, it is fairly unlikely that you will select a printer that Quattro Pro for Windows is unable to cope with. You will be able to use any printer that is classified as Windows compatible.

1.10 The keyboard and mouse

Most keyboards are fairly standard. Before starting, examine your keyboard to determine the whereabouts of the following:

Number pads On most keyboards there are two sets of number keys from 0 to 9 — one set above the QWERTY letters and the other as a number pad to the right side of the keyboard. The reason for this is that some users prefer to use the number pad on the keyboard in the same way they would use a standard calculator. If you do want to use the number pad you will need first to press the **Num Lock** key.

Function Keys These are especially programmed to perform certain functions. On most keyboards they are either along the top or grouped together on the left-hand side. Each key is labelled F1, F2, F3, etc. You will, in time, find some of these very useful when using the Quattro Pro package.

Insert, Home, Page Up, Page Down, Delete, End These exist on most keyboards and, along with the function keys, offer ways of taking shortcuts. These keys will perform different functions depending upon the package in use. Quattro Pro for Windows makes full use of these keys.

↑   ↓   →   ←
Arrow keys (up), (down), (right), (left) These often appear as separate function keys on keyboards. If they do not, then you will have to use the ones that appear on the number pad.

* (Multiplication) This appears above the number 8 key near the top of your keyboard. It is used in order to avoid confusion with the conventional symbol for multiplication '×'. Similarly, / (forward slash) is used for division. So, 8*4 means 8 multiplied by 4; 8/4 means 8 divided by 4.

Ctrl (Control) This will always be used in conjunction with another key. For example, holding down the Ctrl key and pressing the character 'C' (referred to as Ctrl+C) is used in the Windows environment for copying information.

Alt This is used in a similar way to the Ctrl key in that it is pressed simultaneously with other keys to provide a variety of other facilities. For example Alt+F4 is used to quit Quattro Pro for Windows.

Esc (Escape) This key is used rather like a function key and is often used, as is the case in Quattro Pro, to 'back track' on a sequence of events or to 'undo' an activity.

PrtScr (Print Screen) This allows you to 'dump' a copy of the screen to your printer or to the Clipboard. The Clipboard is a part of your computer's internal memory that can be recalled at a later stage.

/ (Forward slash) This key is important when working with Quattro Pro for Windows. Remember to distinguish from \ (back slash). The forward slash is used as a division symbol in most applications.

Getting to know your keyboard is important. However, you will find that if you are new to computing this will take quite some time so you need to be patient. Progress can be slow when you are learning a new package such as Quattro Pro and discovering your keyboard at the same time.

Computers now come equipped with a pointing device called a **mouse** which offers an alternative to the keyboard for performing actions. The mouse is moved around on a flat surface, often on a mouse mat, and interacts with a small cursor that appears on the screen. The pointer can be positioned on an **icon**, a small picture indicating an option available with the aid of a mouse, and when the mouse is 'clicked', by pressing the left of two buttons, a selected action is activated. Such icons are common features when working with Windows and the mouse will be used frequently in this book.

1.11 Data storage on disk

It has already been mentioned that data can be stored on both hard and floppy disks. Such data, however, has to be organised in a way that can be understood by the user and the computer. Data will be collected and stored in **files**. For now, it is simply good enough to know into what kind of files data are organised. There are three types of file that Quattro Pro for Windows users need to know about.

1   Operating system files contain the software that the computer needs to instruct it how to work. These files will appear on the hard disk before the Quattro Pro package is ever introduced.

2   Applications software files will be large in number and the

process of placing such files on to the hard disk is called installing the application.

3 Data keyed in by the user will be placed in one of the sub-directories. For each spreadsheet, for example, there will be a file with its own name, chosen by the user.

Disks, both floppy and hard, have a root directory which acts as a starting-point from which sub-directories are created and into which files are stored.

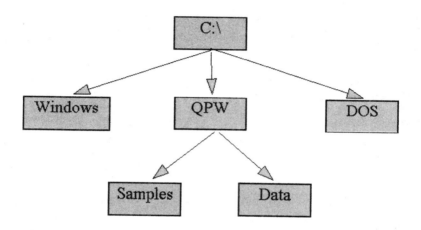

Table 1.1

In Table 1.1 it can be seen that the root directory C: contains three sub-directories: Windows, QPW, DOS. Quattro Pro for Windows files are stored in the QPW sub-directory. The table also shows that the QPW sub-directory has two further sub-directories of samples and data. Organising files in directories is part of the process of file management. In many ways, it is no different from organising files in a filing cabinet. The art of good file management is one of knowing where to find information quickly and efficiently.

1.12 Computer memory

Computer memory is the memory which exists inside the computer other than on disk. Some computer memory is required in order to store programs that are needed to control the computer system – the operating system. Much more memory is needed for two other main purposes.

1 To hold the application software when it is in use. Quattro Pro for Windows is a large software package made up of a great number of separate files all stored on hard disk. Not all of the package is loaded into memory at any one time; this is done only when it is needed. Quattro Pro will frequently load files into memory to instruct it what to do in certain circumstances and then dispose of this from memory when it is no longer required.

2 To hold data generated by the package itself. Again, not all data generated will need to be held in memory at any one time; it will be stored in many separate files and saved on disk.

The size of your computer memory (RAM – for Random Access Memory) is limited. Interacting with files stored on disk allows a computer to extend its capabilities considerably. It is important when buying software that you make sure your machine has enough memory in the computer itself to cope with the version of Quattro Pro you are buying. This is especially important when buying Quattro Pro for Windows. For Version 5.0 you will need a minimum of 4MB of RAM.

1.13 Menus

You will often come across the term 'menu' when working with computers. A menu is simply a list of options that you can choose from. Quite often when selecting a menu option you are given yet more options from that option – a sub-menu. This hierarchical structure of menus is now very common among applications on computers. In practice, the successful use of computer software often largely rests with the operator knowing his or her way around a set of menus.

A good deal of your effort in teaching yourself Quattro Pro will be in finding your way around the Quattro Pro menu structure. Chapter 11 has a special section showing the Quattro Pro menu structure that will prove a useful guide to helping you find your way through the menus when you are at a later stage in this book and beyond.

As mentioned earlier, there are now different versions of the Quattro Pro package. Later versions tend to have a greater number of facilities. Borland has kept the original style and philosophy of the spreadsheet (worksheet) handling. It has achieved this largely by adding the extra functions and inserting more options into the menu structure. This has the clear advantage that if you move from one version of Quattro Pro to another you will be familiar with the style and may only need to learn some new options. In fact when 'upgrading' from one version to another all the data files generated in the earlier version can be used in the new version.

——— 1.14 Installing Quattro Pro ———

When your software arrives you will receive:

● A number of floppy disks containing your software

● A reference manual

● A tutorial manual

● A set of instruction manuals one of which is a book on setting up Quattro Pro on to your computer.

If your hard disk has been prepared in the correct way then the whole process of installing Quattro Pro on to a hard disk has been made a little easier by Quattro Pro as Borland supplies an installation program on one of the floppy disks. What the installation program will achieve is to place the required files from floppy disk on to your hard disk in the correct directories.

Assuming you have a hard disk system or are using a network, then to install the software all you need to do is:

● Switch on your computer and start Windows.

● Insert Disk 1 into drive A;

● Using your mouse, select the File option from the Windows manager menu. Then select Run and type in A:INSTALL.EXE

A set of instructions will appear on the menu guiding you through the installation procedures. When a package like Quattro Pro for Windows is purchased it is done on the understanding that it is for the use of the company or person who purchased it and you will be required to enter the details of such a company. This forms part of the opening screen details when the package is loaded.

The rest of the installation procedure will require you simply to state where you want your spreadsheet software stored. As this package is a Windows based application, Quattro Pro for Windows will know a good deal about your system by the way the Windows software has been set up. For example, it will know what printers are on the system and what they are.

Follow the instructions as they appear; they are largely self-explanatory. You will need to have all the other disks at hand. Eventually you will leave the installation program and will find yourself back at the original window with the new Quattro Pro for Windows icon appearing and all ready for you to run.

If you have installed the software incorrectly, then you can always re-install it. To do this you can run the install program again in exactly the same way as you did before. If you re-run install or wish to make alterations to the way you installed the package in the first instance, you may not need to use all the disks again. Such installation procedures may be needed again if, for example, you change your printer.

—— 1.15 Getting started ——

With the diversity of operating systems and the different versions of Quattro Pro it is very difficult to give precise instructions about installing the package in a book like this. However, once installed, the rest is a little more straightforward.

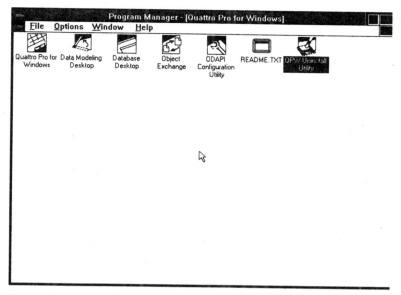

Screen dump 1.2

If you have just installed Quattro Pro you may have to re–boot the computer before the program will work. To do this, hold down the Control and Alt keys together and press Delete. To get into Quattro Pro simply point the cursor at the icon labelled 'Quattro Pro for Windows' with your mouse and perform a double click with the mouse to activate the program. **Screen dump 1.2** shows an example of a Windows screen from which you can select Quattro Pro for Windows. Again, this may differ in that some of the added extras will not appear on your screen if you are not a version 5.0 user or have not installed all the other options. There will be a delay when you activate the loading of the spreadsheet because it needs time to determine the computer system environment it is working in. After this short delay you will be placed straight into the spreadsheet and ready to start. The empty spreadsheet you start with will look something like the one shown earlier in **Screen dump 1.1.**

If you are working on a network system then the whole approach to loading Quattro Pro for Windows may be very different in that an opening screen may appear from which you select the Quattro Pro package. Before progressing to the next chapter you are strongly advised to familiarise yourself with how to enter your particular set up of Quattro Pro, as variations on how to get started can be quite considerable.

——— 1.16 Chapter summary ———

In this chapter you have covered the following points:

- What a spreadsheet is and what it can do

- What software is and what hardware is needed to run Quattro Pro for Windows

- The way data are stored in files and how directory listings are used to give details about the nature of files

- How a hierarchical directory structure can be used to manage the file storage on a disk

- How to install Quattro Pro for Windows and how to open a spreadsheet.

2

STARTING WITH SPREADSHEETS

2.1 Aims of this chapter

The aim of this chapter is to help you get some idea of what a spreadsheet does and its style of operation. Most activities will be by examples as a way of investigating the capabilities of the Quattro Pro package.

To begin with, it is assumed that you have installed Quattro Pro on to your machine. If you have not done so, then refer to the sections in Chapter 1 on Installing Quattro Pro for Windows.

2.2 A blank spreadsheet

● Switch on your machine and make sure you are in Windows and have the Quattro Pro for Windows icon displayed.

● Select the Quattro Pro for Windows icon by positioning your mouse pointer over it and double clicking the left mouse button.

● Once into the application you should see the blank spreadsheet illustrated in **Screen dump 2.1** with cell location A1 highlighted.

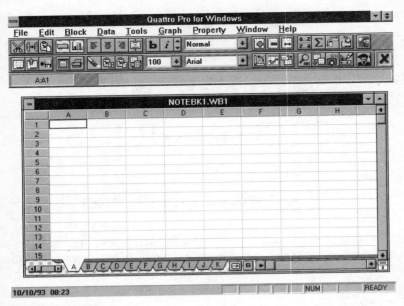

Screen dump 2.1

The display screen

Begin by examining **Screen dump 2.1**

The empty spreadsheet you start off with will vary slightly according to which version of Quattro Pro for Windows you are using and the way you have installed it. These possible variations will not affect your ability to work through the rest of this chapter and beyond.

The arrow that appears on the spreadsheet is controlled by the mouse and moves around the screen as you move your mouse. It is possible to perform everything in the spreadsheet without a mouse, but this will prove inconvenient in the earlier stages of learning how to use spreadsheets.

The control panel

The lines above the spreadsheet (or Notebook) area form the control panel. The top line simply informs you of the package you are in. The second line is a menu bar giving 9 different menu options. This menu will allow you to perform a whole host of actions with your spreadsheet which you will work with through this book. The third line (and fourth line if you are a version 5.0 user) shows a collection of icons on a bar and is called a speed bar. You will click on these icons with the mouse to make time-saving short-cuts. The line just above the notebook area is where you will see your typing – called an input line. If Quattro Pro prompts you for data you will see it here.

In the bottom right corner is the word 'READY' which indicates that the spreadsheet is waiting for input of data. This whole line is known as the status line. The text 'NUM' shows that the number pad to the right of the keyboard has the number lock on and is ready for use. If CAP is showing on your status line then it means that the Caps Lock key on your keyboard has been pressed.

Between the top control panel and the bottom status line appears the Notebook Window which is the working area of the spread-sheet itself. At the bottom of this window appears a set of letters A, B, C, . . . etc. These letters will be used to allow you to jump between different PAGES of your spreadsheet with the use of your mouse. What Quattro Pro is showing you on your screen is simply one page. Quattro Pro allows you to set up to 256 such pages. Almost all the work in this book will work in just the one page, with a separate chapter set aside for the idea of multiple pages in a spreadsheet. For reference, however, you are on the top page referred to as A Page. Some of the other buttons will be explained to you when you will actually benefit from using them.

──────── 2.3 Columns and rows ────────

The letters A, B, C, D, E, F, G, H that appear across the top of the spreadsheet screen below the control panel (referred to by Quattro Pro as the Notebook Window) indicate the column titles, while the numbers 1 to 15 down the left side indicate the rows. The high-lighted part of the screen is situated at location Column A Row 1, referred to as cell A1. You can navigate (move) from cell to cell by moving the pointer with the mouse and clicking the left-hand button to highlight the cell, or you can move from cell to cell with the arrow keys on the keyboard.

● Press the Down Arrow key twice and the Right Arrow key once.

This should leave the cell pointer at cell B3. Look at the input line of the control panel to confirm this. Also the cell should be highlighted with a box.

● Press your Home key to return to cell A1.

The entire spreadsheet is too large to fit on to your screen because there are 256 columns (lettered A, . . . Z, AA, AB, . . . BA, BB to IV) and 8192 rows (numbered 1...8192). However, it is easy to move to any part of the spreadsheet that you need to get to without having to press the arrow keys as the next section will show.

The rectangular bar that highlights the position of the current cell will be referred to as the **cell pointer.**

– 2.4 Moving around the spreadsheet –

The pointer can be moved around the spreadsheet from cell to cell with cursor control keys as shown. First, you can request a cell location by pressing function key **F5**, typing in the cell location you want to move to, and pressing the **Enter** key.

● Press function key F5, type T100, then press the Enter key.

You will now find yourself looking at a part of the spreadsheet not normally visible on the screen.

● Press the **Home** key on your keyboard to return to cell A1, sometimes referred to as the Home position.

● Point the mouse arrow at a cell visible on your screen and press the left mouse button. The cell pointer will then move into the cell. This is the quickest way of moving around the screen.

You can also move the whole section seen on the screen using another set of keys:

PgDn or **Page Down**	Moves one screen down
PgUp or **Page Up**	Moves one screen up
Tab →	Moves one screen to the right
Hold down **Shift**, then press **Tab**	Moves one screen to the left

● Use the keys listed above to get yourself familiar with navigating around the spreadsheet.

● Press the **Home** key on your keyboard to return to cell A1.

Moving the cell pointer off the end of the displayed spreadsheet either vertically or horizontally is known as **scrolling**. As you scroll so new columns or row labels will appear and others will disappear. However, you will always be able to get back to them, and remember information out of sight is not lost.

Another key to help you get around your spreadsheet is the **End** key. If you hold down the End key then press the Down Arrow key you will go to the end of the spreadsheet. If you hold down the End key then press the Right Arrow key you will go to the far right of the spreadsheet.

Finally, you can use your mouse to move around the spreadsheet. In **Screen dump 2.2** you will see the cell pointer in cell IV8192, reached using the End key and the arrow keys, as described in this section.

Beyond the cells on the right-hand side there is a scroll bar with a square box that moves up and down between the two arrows.

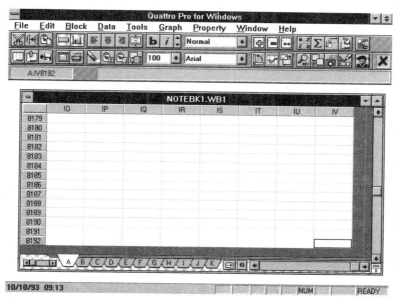

Screen dump 2.2

● Position the mouse arrow on the small box, hold down the left button of your mouse, and slide the box up or down the line. When you let go of the button, the position of the spreadsheet rows will alter accordingly.

There is a similar **scroll bar** to the bottom right-hand side of the Notebook area which allows you to move along the columns in the spreadsheet in a similar way. Sliding these boxes up and down or left and right as a way of getting around the spreadsheet will be particularly useful when spreadsheets become very large.

2.5 Entering text

You can enter four types of data into a cell.

1 **A Number**. This is data of numeric value which can be used in calculations. You will see later in the book that other data, for example, percentage signs, can also be typed in.

2 **A Label.** This is essentially text such as names, addresses and sentences. Such text can contain numbers or any type of character that appears on your keyboard. A label must start with one of the following:

● a letter of the alphabet

● ' (an apostrophe)

● " (a double quote)

● ^ (a caret – normally **Shift** 6)

● \ (a back slash)

Each of these prefixed characters has a different effect on how the text appears in the cell, which you will discover in due course, along with a few others.

3 **A Formula**. This allows you to produce calculations from what else appears in cells in other parts of the spreadsheet. A formula must start with either:

● + (a plus sign) or

● = (an equals sign)

or must be typed between round brackets.

4 **A Function**. This is a built-in formula for mathematical, statistical, financial and other work. Functions begin with a @ sign. An example of such a function is:

@SUM(B3..D5)

which would add up all numeric values in cells B3 to D5.

At this point you should be faced with an empty spreadsheet and should position the cell pointer in cell A1.

Anything you type will first be shown in the input line, below the rows of icons above the notebook area.

Now proceed with the instructions as follows, keeping an eye on what is happening on your screen.

● Type MY FIRST DEMONSTRATION and Press **Enter**.

● Press the Down Arrow key twice, type PRICE and then again press the Down Arrow key. Note how this last action entered the text *and* moved down to the next cell.

● Type COST then press the Down Arrow key.

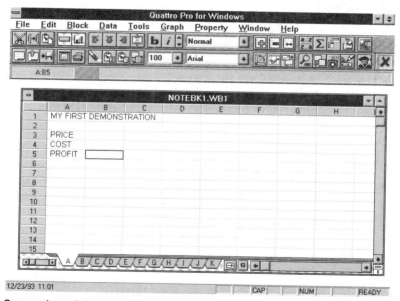

Screen dump 2.3

Such entries of text into cells are referred to as labels. You will no doubt have noticed that these labels always appear left justified (in the far left-hand side of the cell). **Screen dump 2.3** shows what you should have at this stage.

You should be able to see on the screen that the label 'MY FIRST DEMONSTRATION' has been written across adjacent cells. This is permissible only because nothing else appears in these adjacent cells.

———— 2.6 Correcting errors ————

However careful you are, mistakes are going to be made. There are two basic ways of correcting a cell entry. Suppose that the entry 'MY FIRST DEMONSTRATION' was meant to read 'MY FIRST QUATTRO PRO DEMONSTRATION'. To alter it you can position the cursor at cell A1 and simply type the correct label in as though the cell was empty. This will replace the old text with the new entry. Alternatively, you can use a function key to edit the cell contents.

● Position the cell pointer at cell A1 and press the function key **F2**.

● Use the Left Arrow key to move back along the text until you are positioned at the start of DEMONSTRATION. An alternative way could be to position the mouse pointer in front of the word DEMONSTRATION and press the left button of the mouse.

● Now type QUATTRO and press the **Enter** key.

When the text appears in the control panel in this way, you can use other editing keys such as the Right Arrow key and the **back space** keys. This technique can be particularly time-saving when the text is long.

You will see that any type of cell contents can be edited in this way.

You can bypass the use of the function key **F2** by simply pointing your mouse pointer at the text in the Input line on the control panel, clicking your mouse and making the alteration.

───── 2.7 Entering numbers ─────

Quattro Pro distinguishes between VALUES and LABELS simply
through the first character. If the first character is a number (0 to 9)
then a value is assumed, while if the first character is alphabetic
then a label is assumed. Hence, if you type 'Over 18 years of age'
Quattro Pro assumes this to be a label. If, however, you were to
type '18 and over' Quattro Pro would register an input or syntax
error as it would not be able to understand what it believes is a
number. To get Quattro Pro to accept such a string of characters
that begins with a numeric character, you must use ' (apostrophe)
as the first character.

● Now type numbers into each of the cell B3 and B4. Do this by
simply placing the cell pointer into each cell and typing, in turn,
the number 69 in cell B3 and 60 in cell B4. On each occasion
you must press the Enter key, or move the highlighted cell
using the arrow keys.

Such numeric entries will be referred to as VALUES.

───── 2.8 Entering a formula ─────

Position the cell pointer in cell B5 and type +B3–B4 and press the
Enter key.

You have now entered a formula.

Note that this could also have been typed in as =B3–B4 **or** as
(B3–B4).

The calculation of cell B3 minus cell B4 (69 – 60) now appears in
cell B5. The input line in the control panel shows the formula; the
cell shows the result.

This demonstrates how the appearance on the spreadsheet alone
will not reveal what is actually in the cells.

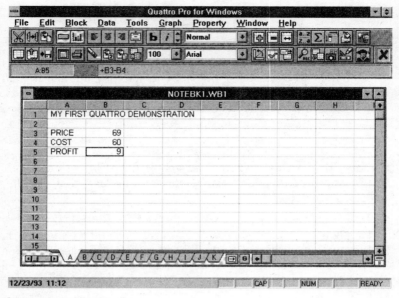

Screen dump 2.4

If you observe **Screen dump 2.4** you will notice that the formula itself appears on the input line while the result of the formula appears in the cell.

It is worth noting that cell references in formulae are not case sensitive; in other words, +b3–b4 reads exactly the same as +B3–B4.

At this stage you will have a spreadsheet with labels in cells A1, A3 and A4; values in cells B3 and B4; and a formula in cell B5. On a very small scale this is what spreadsheets are all about.

Try altering the price and cost cell, preferably moving from cell to cell with the aid of your mouse to position the cell pointer. Before going any further, experiment by creating more cell entries with extra formulae. For example, add a new cell that shows the profit percentage over selling price

+B5/B3*100.

A summary of the special characters to use in formulae would now be useful:

+ Add
− Subtract
* Multiply
/ Divide
(Open bracket (rounded bracket only)
) Close bracket (rounded bracket only)

Building up a formula in Quattro Pro conforms to all the normal rules of mathematical formulae.

──── 2.9 Saving your work ────

In order to save your spreadsheet you will need to select the Save option from the menu at the top of the screen.

● Select the option by positioning the mouse pointer over the menu bar option File and press the left mouse button to see the sub-menu 'pulled down' over that part of the screen.

Such menus are called pull-down menus because you appear to pull the menus down from the top of the screen.

● If you do not have a mouse, then select the menu by holding down the **Alt** key and pressing the first character of the menu option required that is underlined, in this case F. Holding down the **Alt** key and pressing the F key will produce the pull-down menu that you produced using the mouse.

Screen dump 2.5 shows the menu that you will see on your screen. The option you want is 'Save As'. This allows you to save your work in a file with a name of your choice. The other options will be explained later in the book.

● Clicking on the option with your mouse or by using the Down Arrow key or by pressing the A key (the underlined character in the option) select Save As.

At this stage, a Dialogue Box will appear that requires you to enter details about the file; namely, its name and where on your system it is to be placed. As most of the settings should be correct, it is simply enough for you just to type in a file name and press the Enter key.

● Now type in a filename. Give it the name FIRSTGO by typing this in and pressing the Enter key.

As an alternative to pressing the **Enter** key you could use the green Tick button by positioning your mouse point over it and clicking your mouse.

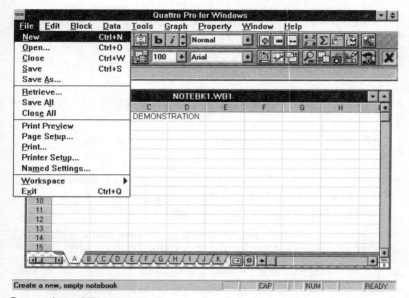

Screen dump 2.5

When you save your work, Quattro Pro automatically gives the file an extension name: .WB1. It has also saved the file in a directory for you.

When you have taken quite some time to develop a spreadsheet of some sophistication, you will need this facility as opposed to re-writing the spreadsheet each time you need it.

———— 2.10 Printing your work ————

To complete the process, you can print the spreadsheet.

If you do not have a printer installed, then skip this section.

● Click on the File option from the menu bar. Then select the Print option from the pull-down menu.

● Alternatively, if you prefer not to use the mouse, then select the commands by holding down the **Alt** key and pressing F followed by P for Print.

In time the various print options will be explained. For now you will use the shortest and easiest commands.

Screen dump 2.6 illustrates the dialogue box that appears. The boxes that need completing require details about pages to be printed and the block to be printed.

Quattro Pro defines 'chunks' of the spreadsheet as BLOCKS. You are asked to define the block you want to print. Later versions of Quattro Pro (including version 5.0) work out the block to be printed based on which cells have data in them. Whether or not the block to be printed *has* been defined for you, it is still worth while working through the next stage in defining exactly what has to be printed. For this purpose, the mouse will be very useful.

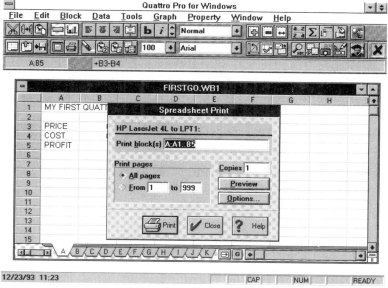

Screen dump 2.6

● Place the mouse pointer on the Print block(s) box where the block to be printed is shown and type in: A1..B6.

This defines the block as the area bounded by the cells A1 to B6. It may well have already been done by Quattro Pro for you as it knows what parts of the spreadsheet have data in them.

● Now click on the Print icon button.

This should start your printer. Meanwhile, on screen you will return to the spreadsheet. If an error has occurred, then it is probably because your printer was not on line or the computer does not have a printer installed. You can still work with Quattro Pro, but you will not be able to print out your work.

If no error message has appeared and your printer has not printed, then it may be because the output has been stored in a file for printing later from the Print Manager in Windows. If this is the case, then you will have to return to Windows and activate the Print Manager. Refer to your Windows manual or to *Teach Yourself Windows* for help.

To do all this more quickly using the mouse:

● Return to the spreadsheet by leaving the menu. This should be the state you are at when you have finished printing. If not press the **Esc** key on your keyboard.

● Click on cell A1 and, keeping the left mouse button depressed, move the pointer to the right and downwards. The area changes colour. When you take your finger off the mouse button the area remains this different colour and has now become highlighted. Highlight the block of 15 squares as in Screen dump 2.7.

Screen dump 2.7 shows the effect of having the required block highlighted before requesting printed output. This method of highlighting blocks prior to using a command will be adopted as a common approach to getting things done.

At this point you can click on the File and Print options from the pull-down menus again and select Print, or simply click on the Print icon.

Defining a block in this way will prove essential in future chapters and in developing efficient use of spreadsheets; hence it is important to spend time on getting it right.

If you have not been able to follow all of this or feel unable to remember how everything was achieved, then do not worry. You will get further help and practice as you work through the book.

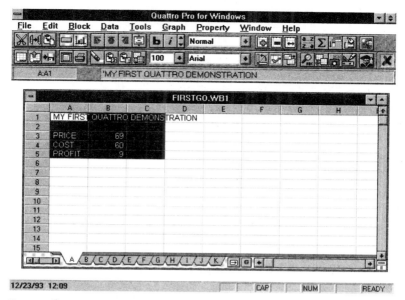

Screen dump 2.7

You will now have performed the typical process involved in producing a spreadsheet, namely:

1 Opening Quattro Pro for Windows.

2 Preparing a spreadsheet with Labels, Values and Formulae.

3 Entering a varied number of values to see what the results would be.

4 Saving the spreadsheet in a file with a filename.

5 Highlighting the block in the spreadsheet.

5 Printing the highlighted spreadsheet.

-2.11 Erasing data from a spreadsheet-

To produce a more sophisticated spreadsheet, erase the existing one.

● Highlight the cells that contain data.

● Select from the menu bar the option Edit.

● From the pull-down menu, select the option Clear Contents.

The highlighted block will have cleared.

This method of clearing data can be useful if you have made a mistake and wish to re-enter a number of cell entries. Always save the spreadsheet first before deleting anything.

There are other ways of deleting blocks of data, such as deleting specified rows or columns, which will be explained at a later stage in the book.

— 2.12 A new spreadsheet – sales — performance

It is now time to produce a more sophisticated spreadsheet similar to that shown in **Screen dump 2.8**.

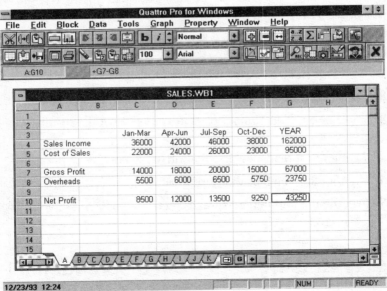

Screen dump 2.8

The text and data will have to be typed in as you would do with a word processor. The calculations of Gross Profit, Net Profit and Totals are made by Quattro Pro.

- Click on cell C3 and type the quarter-yearly heading: Jan–Mar.

- Using the Right Arrow move to cell D3 and type: Apr–Jun.

- Continue with Jul–Sep in cell E3, Oct–Dec in cell F3, and YEAR in cell G3.

If you want to enter text into a cell and centre it within that cell rather then leave it left-justified, then you should prefix the text with the ^ (caret) sign. **NOTE:** This method of centring text should not be done with the numbers, as Quattro Pro will not recognise the cell entry as a number and so cannot use it for calculations.

- Now type the other labels required: Sales Income in cell A4, Cost of Sales in A5, Gross Profit in cell A7, Overheads in cell A8 and Net Profit in cell A10.

- Now type the data for Sales Income and Cost of Sales for each of the four quarters (8 numbers in total).

All the remaining figures will be calculated by Quattro Pro using formulae that you will type in.

- Click on cell C7 and type in the formula +C4–C5. When you press the **Enter** key the correct figure for Gross Profit should appear. i.e. Sales Income less Cost of Sales.

Instead of entering the formulae for the remaining quarters, you will use a different technique.

- Click on G5, type @SUM(C5..F5) and press the **Enter** key. This adds up all the Cost of Sales figures.

- In cell G4 type in a function for adding up the Sales Income figures: @SUM(C4..F4).

Now you will use the copying facility to copy the formula that appears in cell C7 to appear in the cells D7 to G7.

- Click on cell C7 because this is the cell containing the formula you want to copy.

- Select from the menu bar the option Edit and then from the pull-down menu the option Copy.

Although nothing appears to have happened, Quattro Pro has placed the cell contents into the system Clipboard. This is a part of the memory that is used to store data on a temporary basis. What is needed now is to Paste this into the spreadsheet.

● Highlight the block D7 to G7 using your mouse. To achieve this, click the mouse pointer at cell D7 and, holding the left mouse button down, drag the pointer to cell G7 and let the mouse button go.

● Now select from the menu bar the option Edit and then from the pull-down menu the option Paste.

It should now be apparent that the method and principle of high-lighting a block of cells is an important one to be familiar with as it is used to save a considerable amount of keyboard work.

The next stage is to type in a formula for the Overhead figures. For this purpose it has been assumed that Overheads are to be 25% of Cost of Sales. Given this assumption, proceed as follows:

● Click on cell C8 and type in the formula: +C5*25%.

Note how 25% is recorded as 0.25 in the formula that appears on the Input line below the icons. Note also that the correct figure of 5500 appears in the cell.

Do not use the copy command just yet because there is an even better way of saving time.

Net Profit is Gross Profit less Overheads.

● Click on cell C10, type in the formula: +C7–C8, and press the Enter key.

The next stage will be to copy both the Overheads formula and the Net Profit formula for the other quarters and for the year – in a single action.

● Highlight the block of cells C8 to C10.

● Now select from the menu bar the option Edit and then from the pull-down menu the option Copy.

● Highlight the block of cells D8 to G10. This will define a block of three rows and four columns.

● Select from the menu bar option Edit and then Paste.

This has enabled you to copy two sets of formulae in a single operation. What you have now done is fundamental to making spreadsheet handling quick and easy to set up. If you are unclear at this stage about what has happened, then give yourself time to experiment.

This now completes the spreadsheet. At this stage you should experiment by changing some of the numbers (not the formulae). If you change some of the quarterly Sales Income figures or Cost of Sales figures, the rest of the spreadsheet will adjust by recalculating Gross Profit, Overheads, Net Profits and Year totals.

● Now print and save the spreadsheet as you did in the previous section of this chapter, remembering the sequence of events:

(If necessary, highlight what you want printed)
Click on the Print icon
Click on the green tick

● Save your spreadsheet by selecting from the menu bar the option File, then Save <u>A</u>s, typing in: SALES, and clicking **OK**.

2.13 Asking for help

At any time while working through a spreadsheet, Quattro Pro offers you various levels of help. You can get help by pressing

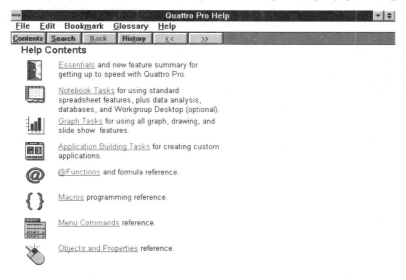

Screen dump 2.9

function key F1. Doing this produces a screen similar to the one in **Screen dump 2.9**.

This screen gives you the contents list of some of the help topics available within Quattro Pro. As you move the mouse pointer through the list a small hand appears over the contents item. You can click on any of these topics and a new page appears. To scroll through the list click on the scroll boxes on the right-hand side of the screen.

You could spend a considerable amount of time looking through the many pages of help available. Pressing the **Esc** key on your keyboard will return you to your spreadsheet at the same position and state you left it.

As mentioned, Quattro Pro has differing levels of help. To see what this means;

● Click on the File option from the menu bar.

● Press function key **F1** or activate the question mark Icon with your mouse.

Now you get a Help screen that tells you what the facilities are in the File pull–down menu.

● Press the **Esc** key to return to the spreadsheet.

● Click on Save option to save your most recent changes.

When you repeat a Save option like this, you will be reminded that a file with that name has already been saved. You will be given the chance either to **Replace** the current one with what is already on your disk, **Create** a backup copy, or **Cancel** the entire operation.

● In response to the message that the File already exists and after you have seen the Help screen, select the **Replace** option.

● Finally, select from the File menu the option Exit to return to your Windows screen.

The results of the actions in this chapter are, therefore, to have created two spreadsheets which have been saved on your disk and can be Retrieved at a later stage.

———— 2.14 Chapter Summary ————

You have covered the following points:

● How to load Quattro Pro for Windows.

● How to identify the control panel, the menu bar, and the icons at the top of the screen.

● How to move around or navigate the spreadsheet in a variety of different ways.

● How to highlight cells.

● How to distinguish different types of cell entries: labels, numbers, formulae, and functions.

● How to correct typing errors.

● How to use the menu bar and the pull-down menus.

● How to define and highlight Blocks.

● How to use options the Edit pull-down menu to copy and to erase blocks of cells.

● How to Print spreadsheets.

● How to use File commands Save, Save As, and Exit.

● How to use the Help pages.

3

MENUS, PRINTING __ AND FILING

3.1 Aims of this chapter

One of the principal features of getting to know any software package is being able to find your way around the menu system. Quattro Pro for Windows is no exception to this. It has a hierarchical structure of menus which you have already encountered. The first level appears across the menu bar near the top of your screen, with the next level pulled down when you implement it. Further levels are then produced as you implement further options. This chapter will make you more familiar with the menu structure and help you understand the main options you will commonly need when using the spreadsheet.

In describing the menu system, emphasis has been placed on saving and retrieving files to and from your hard disk as well as being able to print your spreadsheet.

Three of the menus described in this chapter are activated by using your mouse, particularly the right hand button of your mouse. Such actions create an **Object Inspector** on your screen – a dialogue box of parameters to set.

Although these were all introduced in the previous chapter, this chapter investigates these facilities in much more detail.

3.2 Changing the style of your spreadsheet

You have already been introduced to how to write and save a file. Reproduce the spreadsheet depicted in **Screen dump 3.1**. The spreadsheet contains no formulae or functions, just labels and numbers. You will notice that column A is not wide enough to hold the label Wednesday; leave it as it stands for now because you will learn how to widen the cell.

Screen dump 3.1

Before saving the file, you will use the menu structure to set all numbers in the spreadsheet to two decimal places and to widen column A. The first step before saving the file will be to format all numbers to two places of decimals. This involves altering the style of the spreadsheet.

● Highlight the block of cells where the numbers are stored: B6 to E11.

As explained in the previous chapter, this defines the block you want to work with.

● Click on the Edit option from the menu bar.

● From here select the Define Style option that appears near the bottom of the Edit options listed.

At this stage an object inspector will appear. You will come across these object inspectors many more times as they are used to alter the appearance of your spreadsheet. What is needed at the moment is the Format option.

● From the object inspector, select the Format option by placing your mouse pointer over the Format button and clicking.

At this stage you should have **Screen dump 3.2** which shows the layers of menus.

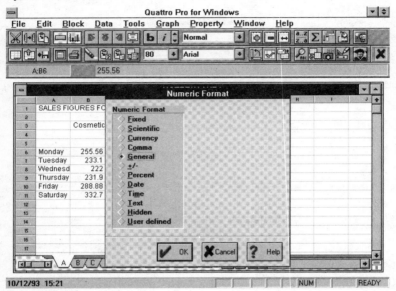

Screen dump 3.2

● From the list of available formats click on the one called Fixed using your mouse.

A new box appears showing the number of decimal places as 2. This can be altered if required. However, the settings are correct in that the default of 2 decimal places is required and the block has already been set.

● Click on the green Tick from the object inspector to return to the original object inspector for defining style.

● Now click on the green Tick again to see the outcome. Next, you should widen column A so that the whole of Wednesday can be seen. Quattro Pro starts off with all columns set to 9 characters wide. You will need to have column A at least 11 characters wide. There are three ways to set the column width. The method used here will help you find your way around the menus, but an easier way will be shown later.

● Position the cell pointer at any cell in column A.

● Now press the right button on your mouse to reveal a different object inspector.

● If you are a version 5.0 user, then you should select the Block Properties option from the list of options to reveal the correct object inspector.

The object inspector here is not a great deal different from the one you saw before except it has more options, of which Column Width is one. In fact, you can use this menu for altering the appearance on your spreadsheets instead of the Edit pull-down menu from the menu bar. You will soon discover that to achieve many obstacles in Quattro Pro, there is often more than one technique.

● Now click on the Column Width option from the column of options shown on the left side of the object inspector.

An object inspector will appear on your screen similar to that show in **Screen dump 3.3**.

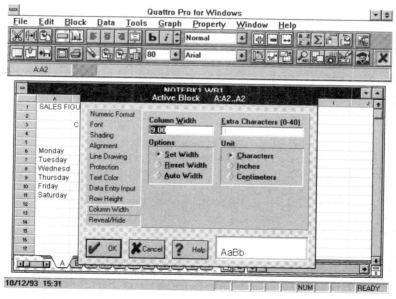

Screen dump 3.3

● Type in: 12 in the Set width box, which should show 9.

● Use your mouse to activate the setting by clicking on the green Tick button.

Later you will see how to widen more than one column at a time. Much of this work and other tasks can be performed more quickly using the speedbar icons.

———— 3.3 The menu structure ————

This method of altering the appearance of the spreadsheet will be discussed again on more occasions. You should by now be getting a good appreciation of how the menu structure looks. As a means of summary, the Edit options are depicted in the tree diagram in **Table 3.1**.

When you see the menu structure on your screen you will notice that one character in each option is underlined. This tells you what the single character key is for selecting that option. This method of using a single key depression to select an option from the menu is an alternative to using the mouse or arrow keys to highlight the option required.

You will also notice that some of the options in the menu are in a lighter shade. This indicates that the option is not at present available. For example, if the Paste option is in a light shade, it is because there is nothing in the Clipboard for Quattro Pro to paste on to the spreadsheet.

By examining this tree diagram, you should be able to observe the route taken in order to achieve the objectives of either, say, clearing the contents of a block of cells or inserting an object into the spreadsheet. Although many command sequences will soon become familiar to you, there are some that are so infrequently used that you will have difficulty in remembering them without the aide of such diagrams.

As a further demonstration, you used the right button of your mouse to activate an object inspector for formatting blocks rather than using the Edit pull-down menu from the menu bar. A good deal of use ought to be made of this. **Table 3.2** shows how this is set out.

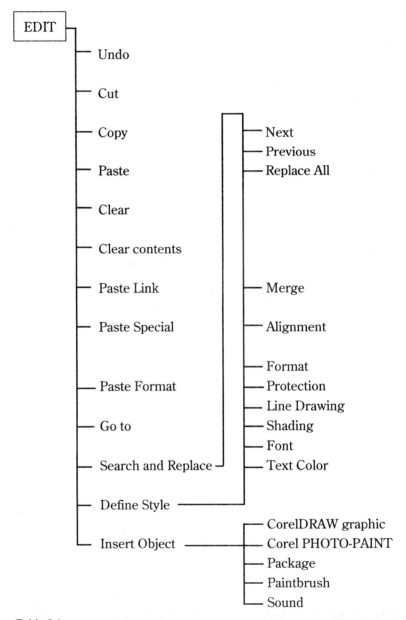

Table 3.1

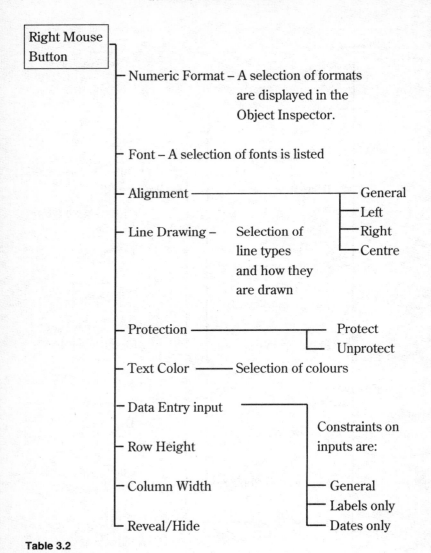

Table 3.2

While working with the menus there will be two main sources of help available to you. First will be the prompts given at the very top of your screen. These prompts will give you basic instructions as to what input is expected. Secondly, you can always seek help by pressing the function key **F1**.

Many of the items in the menu and object inspectors and which appear in the two tables have not been dealt with yet. Most will be covered later in this book. However, once you have become familiar with the items available, you will soon appreciate that finding your way around these menus remains the only real obstacle to speedy spreadsheet work.

3.4 Saving a file

This next section will explain in a little more detail the process of saving your file.

- Click on the File option from the menu bar. Then select the Save <u>A</u>s option, and type in the name STORE.

You will have noticed that there are many options available in the <u>F</u>ile pull-down menu. A little explanation is now in order.

New: This opens a new spreadsheet. When a new spreadsheet is started, an old one remains. You will experiment with this in a later chapter.

Open: This allows you to open a spreadsheet that already exists without losing the one you are currently working with.

Close: This closes the current spreadsheet file. This option will prompt you for a file name if you have not saved the most current version.

Save: This will allow you to save a file that you have either saved before or one that you have retrieved. In other words, it saves the file under the same name previously given. When using this, you will be asked if you want it to replace the previous version or save it as a backup.

Save As: This will save an existing spreadsheet with another file name or will save a spreadsheet that has not previously been saved. You will always be prompted for a file name using this option.

Retrieve: This will open a file and close an existing one if it is opened. If a file is already open and has not had its most recent changes saved, then a dialogue box appears asking if you want the changes lost. If you answer No, then you have the chance to go back and save the changes first.

Save All: This saves all spreadsheet files that are open. Quattro Pro allows you to work on more than one spreadsheet at a time

Close All: This closes all spreadsheet files that are currently open.

The remaining options are related to the printing of your work.

Print Preview: This allows you to see your file as it will appear when it is printed.

Page Setup: This lets you determine the way the spreadsheet will appear when printed. Quattro Pro will set the page layout for you, but this allows you to alter things like headers and footers, orientation, and margins.

Printer Setup: This is used to set up your printer differently from the way it is set up by the Windows printer control.

Print: This prints your specified block of cells.

Named Settings: Quattro Pro allows you to store a set of printer settings that can be called on at a later stage. This means that if you have spend some time setting up various parameters for your printer, you can save them with a name and call on them at a later stage.

Exit: Returns to the Windows screen.

Most of these are not needed in the earlier stages and are there to allow you better to tailor the spreadsheet package to particular needs.

● Having saved your file click on the Close option from the File pull-down menu.

At this point, all you should have is a blank notebook area indicating to you that there is no spreadsheet to work with.

Opening a file is the reverse of saving one.

● Click on File, then Open.

You will now see the Open File dialogue box. If your file does not appear among the titles, then it may be because there is not enough room in the window to display all the available file names. Use the arrow keys to scroll through the file names. As an alternative to the arrow keys, you can use your mouse to move the box between the up and down arrows.

● Select the file saved as STORE by clicking on it with the mouse. Then click on the OK button.

The STORE.WB1 file should now reappear on your screen.

— 3.5 Expanding your spreadsheet —

Now you can add to the spreadsheet. First, type in formulae for the totals in column F.

● Click on cell F6.

● Type in the start of the function: @SUM(

Instead of typing in the block where the numbers are located, you can highlight the block in the same way as you have highlighted blocks before:

● Highlight the block of numbers in row 6 from B6 to E6. Do not press **Enter** at this stage.

● Type in the closing bracket)

● Press Enter to confirm the formula in the cell.

The desired result should be to total the numbers in the columns. Check that this is so. The function in cell F6 should be @SUM(B6..E6). The next objective is to copy this formula to the range F7 to F11.

● Position the cell pointer at cell F6 where the formula has been entered. This is the one you need to copy.

● Click on Edit and select Copy.

This has stored the formula in the Clipboard.

● Highlight the block of cells F7 to F11.

● Click on Edit and select Paste.

You now have daily totals for the complete store. Next you should type in formulae to add up the weekly totals for each department and one for the overall sales of the store.

● Click on cell B13 and type in a formula. The formula is @SUM(B6..B11) but use the highlighting method to define the block).

● Copy the formula in cell B13 to the block C13 to F13.

● Type in a label, right justified, in cell A13 as TOTALS. Remember, to right justify you need to prefix the label with ".

As the figures are quoted in £ sterling, the next stage will be to format all numbers to two places of decimal as currency.

● Highlight the block of cells from B6 to F13.

● Making certain that your mouse pointer is inside the notebook area, click the right button of the mouse to display an object inspector.

● If you are a version 5.0 user, click on the Block Properties option from the list of options.

● From this object inspector make sure the selected option on the far left of the object inspector is set to the Numeric-Format option. Click on the option if this is not so.

● From the options to the right of this, click on Currency.

The remaining settings in the object inspector are as you need them; hence you can leave them as they are.

● Click on the green tick (OK) to activate the format and return to the spreadsheet.

Now you may be presented with a further problem: the figures are probably quoted in dollars ($). If they are quoted in £s then you need not carry out the next activity; although going through the motions will show you how alterations can be made. In order to alter the currency, you will need to use another part of the menu system that is again activated by your mouse.

● Place the mouse pointer at the very top of the screen over the Title bar.

● Now click the right button of your mouse to activate another object inspector.

● Click on the International option on the left side of the object inspector and from there select Currency.

A panel will appear with various settings. If the currency is as you require, then it can be left unaltered. **Screen dump 3.4** shows what the Object Inspector should look like and how the settings should be made.

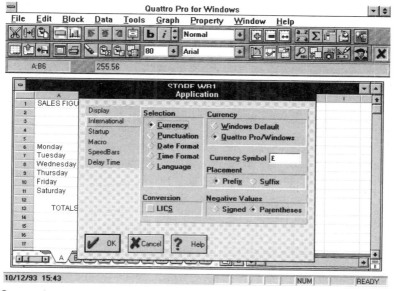

Screen dump 3.4

● Now type in the symbol £ as a replacement for $.

● Quit by clicking on the OK option when you are satisfied that the settings are correct.

You could for instance, alter the currency to other currencies, allowing your spreadsheet to relate to other countries better. For example, if the store was based in Berlin, you can change the currency symbol to DM (Deutschmarks) which would then be suffixed to the numbers.

If some cells have a row of asterisks in them, it is because the cells are not wide enough to display the numbers. This has to be put right by widening the columns.

● Widen the columns so that all numbers can be seen with your mouse. It can be done by moving the mouse pointer to the Column letter at the top of the notebook area and 'dragging' the column width open with your mouse. Hold the pointer to the right of the letter, then keep the left mouse button depressed and move the mouse very slightly to the right.

This technique can be used for altering the size of the spreadsheet on your screen and so is worth spending some time practising with.

Next, you will remove the grid lines that appear on the spreadsheet. To do this, you will activate yet another object inspector with your mouse.

● Place your mouse pointer over the letter A that appears at the bottom of your screen.

The letters that appear at the foot of the Notebook area of your screen are page identifiers. You are at page A.

● With the mouse pointer on 'A' click the right button.

The object inspector that appears allows you to set up Page Properties. The properties are listed on the left side of the object inspector.

● Click on Grid Lines, which is towards the bottom of this list.

● Remove the ticks beside both Horizontal and Vertical by clicking your left mouse button over each tick.

● Click on OK and return to your spreadsheet to observe the outcome.

The spreadsheet should now look similar to that shown in **Screen dump 3.5**.

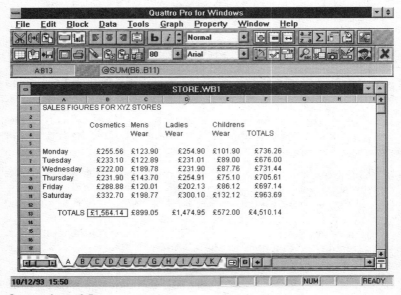

Screen dump 3.5

You can, of course, leave either Vertical or Horizontal lines only using the same approach. Before moving on to the next section, it is now a useful exercise to take a quick peek at what you had before making these additions.

The first stage will be to save your file under a different name:

● Click on File on the menu bar and select Save As.

● Type in the file name STORE2 and select OK.

● From the File pull-down menu, select Open and then, from the list of files, select STORE again.

You now have two copies of the same file of which the last one you opened will be visible on your screen and is the original you started with.

● Pull down the Window menu.

● Select STORE2 from the list of files that appears.

This now presents you with the files open to you to pick from. If you pick STORE2 then you will be returned to that sheet. (In an application of this kind, the store could, for instance, keep a spreadsheet for each week of the year. You could then open different weeks and make various comparisons.)

You can hop back and forth between spreadsheets making alterations to one without affecting the others. You can also work in either spreadsheet without affecting the other. Chapter 10 will show you how you can link formulae between two spreadsheets.

—— **3.6 Relative and absolute cell —— addresses**

At the moment, keep both spreadsheets open and make sure that you have selected the most recently created spreadsheet to work with, namely, STORE2. This section will examine the more advanced features of copying formulae from one part of the spreadsheet to another.

In row 15 you will create a new formula that expresses each Department total as a percentage of the Grand Total. The departmental percentage is the departmental total divided by the overall total expressed as a percentage. In this exercise, you will need to type in a formula in cell B15 to express this figure and then copy the formula across the other departments. The problem with this is that when you copy the formula the relative position of the overall total will alter for each department.

In a formula, a reference to a cell that does not change when you copy the formula is called an **ABSOLUTE** reference. An absolute always refers to the same cell or block. To create an absolute cell reference, type a $ (dollar sign) before the column letter and again before the row number when you write the formula.

● Highlight cell B15 and type in the formula +B13/$F$13.

The result will appear as a decimal and will need to be formatted as a percentage. This will be done later.

● Now copy the cell B15 to the block C15 to E15.

As an exercise, repeat the two steps just undertaken but with the formula +B13/F13 in cell B15. Try to see what has happened by looking at each formula through the block.

Now you need to alter the format so that percentages are shown.

● Highlight the block of cells B15 to E15.

● Making sure you have your mouse pointer in the notebook area, click your right mouse button.

● If you are a version 5.0 user, click on Block Properties.

● Click on Numeric Format to reveal another object inspector.

● Click on the Percent option.

● Set the number of decimal places to 0 (zero).

● Click on the OK button.

As a next task, you will introduce two new departments: Electrical and Furniture. These two new departments will appear between Cosmetics and Men's Wear. To do this, you will need to insert two new columns.

● You should now select where the new columns are to go by first highlighting cells in both columns C and D. Which two cells does not matter.

- Click on the Speedbar the green + (plus) icon.

- On the object inspector you have now activated, ensure the following settings are made:

Dimension set to	Columns
Span set to	Entire

- Click on OK and observe the outcome.

The effect of this has been to insert two columns and to shift the columns to the right two columns along. You will also note that the formulae in all cells have been preserved.

- Now type in the new headings for the Electrical and Furniture departments. Try the following as these numbers will prove useful in the remaining parts of this chapter:

	Electrical	Furniture
Monday	322	0
Tuesday	291	1,200
Wednesday	228.23	100
Thursday	256.12	499.99
Friday	331.2	5,400
Saturday	410.1	12,099

The new numbers entered will have the same format as the numbers in the adjoining cells because Quattro Pro sees it as part of the same block of cells that you originally formatted. This means you will not need to format the new block for currency.

- Widen the new columns sufficiently so that all numbers can be seen.

- To get a different view of the spreadsheet, select New View from the Windows pull-down menu.

Now the end columns are off the screen because the entire spreadsheet does not fit the screen. As a further demonstration of the windows facilities, you will next create a vertical window in column B that allows you to move around the table of figures and be able to see the days of the week stay in the left-most part of the screen.

- Click on a cell in column B.

- Click on Window on the menu bar and then on the Panes option.

- In the Object Inspector click on the Vertical option, then click on the OK button.

You have now split your screen into two windows with both windows showing the same spreadsheet, but at differing points. To move between windows you can press function key **F6** or point your mouse pointer to the window you want to work in and press the mouse button.

To finish the job off, you need to complete the departmental totals and percentages for the two new departments.

- Make sure you are in the right-hand window.

- Now copy the block of cells B13 to B15 to the block C13 to D15, remembering to use the Edit facilities of Copy and Paste.

Notice how not only the formula has copied, but also the formats defined for the cells you have copied from.

- Click on the Window option on the menu bar and from the list of spreadsheets you have open, click on STORE2.WB1:1.

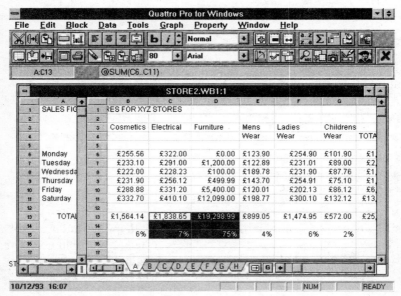

Screen dump 3.6

You will notice from this that Quattro Pro has created an extra spreadsheet with the new perspective. You have the facility to skip between spreadsheets via the Window pull-down menu.

● Create a vertical window in column B again.

At this stage you should have a screen similar to that shown in **Screen dump 3.6.**

——— 3.7 Using a window to see two ——— spreadsheets

Before proceeding any further, it is wise to save your latest efforts again so that nothing is lost.

● Click on File option from the pull-down menu, then click on the Save option, then on Replace.

At this stage you will have saved the current version as STORE2 again. Remember that STORE, which was the earlier version, will also be on disk and is still open.

● From the Window menu click on the Tile option.

You can hop freely between these two spreadsheets by clicking on them in the same way as you hopped between the windows in the same spreadsheet.

From the Window option you can also select Cascade to see the spreadsheets one behind the other. In Chapter 10 you will see how Quattro Pro allows you to set up something similar to this by giving a spreadsheet a three-dimensional effect of multiple sheets within a single spreadsheet.

● Return to the tiled windows.

● Ensure that you are in the old spreadsheet STORE.WB1.

● Close the file by clicking on the File option, then on Close.

This will leave your screen half empty. To use the full screen on your spreadsheet, either:

● Take the mouse pointer gently to the edge of the spreadsheet until you see the pointer become a double-headed arrow.

● Then, holding the mouse button down, drag the mouse to the right to fill up your screen with the spreadsheet, rather like pulling a curtain across a rail.

or:

● Click on the maximise button in the right-hand corner of the line containing the file title.

– 3.8 Fonts, presentation and printing –

The final section of this chapter will investigate the way you can alter the complete look of your spreadsheet. What you are able to achieve here may be a little restricted depending on the capabilities of your screen and printer.

To see more clearly what is going on, close the vertical window to have the whole spreadsheet showing on the screen.

● Click on <u>W</u>indows, then select <u>P</u>anes.

● Now click on Clear from the object inspector to remove the vertical window.

In order to see the whole spreadsheet on your screen you may need to alter the width of some of your columns.

● Go through each of the columns reducing the widths where you can.

● To reduce the widths of more than one column at a time, highlight a block of cells across more than one column. Click your right mouse button and then select, from the Block Properties object inspector, click on the Column width option and set your column width followed by OK.

Next you will have the opportunity to play around with the visual impact of what you have on the screen. This will vary in accordance with your system, so you will be left to experiment for yourself after a few preliminary instructions.

Look at **Screen dump 3.7** to get an idea of what can be achieved. Do not concern yourself if you are unable to get an exact match of this. Your system may either be unable to achieve this or is simply different from the one that was used for the purpose of writing this book.

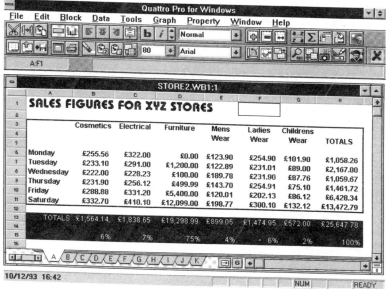

Screen dump 3.7

All of the actions taken to achieve the above has been done with the Quattro Pro object inspector that is activated with the mouse positioned in the notebook area of the screen. The outline of this was set out in Table 3.2 earlier.

First, you should discover the fonts. A font is the style of print that appears. A font can be large or small or, as shown in **Screen dump 3.7**, can be in different styles. There are hundreds of fonts, each with its own name.

To select a font:

● Highlight a block of cells – cell A1, for example.

● Call up the object inspector with the right button of your mouse.

● If you are a version 5.0 user click on Block Properties from the list of options.

● Click on the Font option.

A selection of fonts will be listed on your screen. The numbers accompanying the fonts indicate their size. The standard size is 12 point. You should now observe the object inspector carefully and decide on three things:

Typeface: There will be a long list of these and you may have to scroll down the list to get what you want.

Point size: 12 is the default size. The bigger the number, the bigger the font size.

Options: You can set Bold, Italic, Underline, and Strikeout.

The box in the bottom right of the object inspector shows you what the text would look like with the chosen selections as you work through them.

- Experiment with altering the fonts and observing what they would look like as you go.

- When you are satisfied, select OK to see the effect on your spreadsheet.

Use the alignment to centre the text of the column headings.

- Highlight cells B3 to H4.

- Call up the object inspector with the right button of your mouse and select Alignment.

- Click on the Center box from the object inspector.

- Now click on Font, rather than OK, and choose a font.

- When you are satisfied, click on OK to see the result.

Some of the blocks are boxed. In order to do this for the actual sales figures bounded by the block A13 to H15, try the following.

- Highlight the block A13 to H15.

- Click on Block Properties.

Here you can set up the following:

Line Drawing to produce lines on the outside of the block only, lines on the inside of the block only, or lines around all cells in the block.

- Click on Outside from this to draw a line around the outside and select the thick line.

● Now click on OK.

Blocks can also be shaded and the colours of the background can be changed as well the text.

● Now click on Shading and select the black shade from the Blend boxes. The text will disappear.

The two boxes of colours allow you to select one from each with the blended effect of each of the colours appearing in the Blend panel of colours. This gives you a vast range of different colours to work with.

● Now click on Text Color and change it to white. This will make the block appear black with white text.

This can be fun and you should experiment with this as much as possible. Some of the other options that have not been used yet can also be experimented with. When you have exhausted what you see is available, save your work before going on to print the final product.

Finally, print your spreadsheet.

● Highlight the block where all data are showing.

● Click on File from the menu bar, then Print (or click on the print Icon on your speedbar).

● If any settings are wrong, alter them.

● Click on OK to start printing.

As an alternative to printing, you can always preview the printed spreadsheet on your screen.

● Click on File then Page Preview.

This will show you what the printed output should like. Such a facility can save a good deal of time as it avoids you having to wait for a print-out to see if the effect is what you want, and that the spreadsheet fits on to your paper. It also saves paper.

● Press the **Esc** key to return to the spreadsheet.

This ability of Quattro Pro to give such a good visual presentation will be further developed in the next chapter when you go on to explore graphics. For now, try to spend some more time experimenting with what you have before you.

3.9 Chapter summary

This chapter has concentrated on how Quattro Pro commands are organised in a hierarchical menu structure and the use of object inspectors. Finding your way around menus will become easier though practice and experience.

In both file handling and printing, you will have examined only a part of what can be achieved. However, in both cases you have seen the important principles involved.

In this chapter you have:

● Understood the menu bar, pull-down menus, and the sub-menu structure that is available.

● Understood how a command sequence works.

● Examined the concept via a tree structure.

● Activated three different object inspectors with the right button of your mouse.

● Altered object inspectors settings to suit your needs.

● Widened columns.

● Saved and retrieved files in different ways.

● Used Copy and Paste to copy both relative and absolute formulae.

● Formatted blocks for currency and set the currency symbol.

● Inserted columns.

● Split screens to help you with extra large spreadsheets.

● Used windows to inspect more than one spreadsheet at a time; used Tile and Cascade.

● Altered the physical appearance of a spreadsheet with differing fonts, lines, colours and shading.

● Printed a spreadsheet with graphics-type output.

4

SOME STATISTICS __ AND GRAPHS

───── 4.1 Aims of this chapter ─────

Quattro Pro has an extremely useful graphing facility that is able to put a much finer touch to your data. The purpose of this chapter is to familiarise you with these facilities and to develop your spreadsheet skills further.

Apart from being able to draw graphs, you will see that once the graph has been set up, it is instantly redrawn as the data change. Later in the book, in Chapter 8, you will return to graphs and take the whole process a stage further.

───── 4.2 Entering the statistics ─────

● Open a new spreadsheet by clicking on File, then select New. Look at **Screen dump 4.1** to see what you will be aiming at in terms of the data for the first exercise.

Before moving on, think about how the data are to be set out and, in particular, which data areas are be calculated by Quattro Pro and which are to be typed in by you.

● Click on cell C1, type Borland Street Motors and press the Enter key.

● By way of improving the heading make sure the cell pointer is on cell C1 and, making sure the mouse pointer is in the notebook area, click your right mouse button to reveal the notebook object inspector.

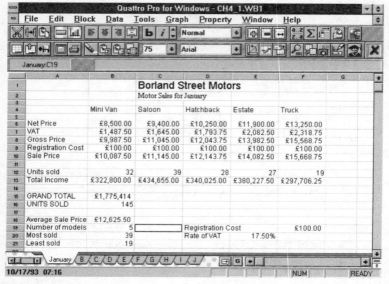

Screen dump 4.1

● If you are a version 5.0 user you will need to click on the Object Properties option.

● Click on Font, increase the point size to 24, and set the text to Bold.

● Click on cell C2 and type Motor Sales for January.

When typing the text into cells, the backspace key allows you to delete characters. Also, if text is already on the spreadsheet and you want it altered, then use the editing facilities of function key **F2** or your mouse to put it right. Altering text in cells will not alter the font setting.

● Start with the following entries:

Cell	Type	Press
B4	Mini Van	Right Arrow
C4	Saloon	Right Arrow
D4	Hatchback	Right Arrow
E4	Estate	Right Arrow
F4	Truck	**Enter**.

- Highlight cells B4 to F4.

- Call up the notebook object inspector again with the right-hand button of your mouse and click on Column Width, (after clicking on Object Properties for version 5.0).

- Click on Auto Width.

- Click on cell A6 and proceed with the following entries:

Cell	Type	Press
A6	Net Price	Down arrow key
A7	VAT	Down arrow key
A8	Gross Price	Down arrow key
A9	Registration Cost	Down arrow key
A10	Sale Price	Down arrow key TWICE
A12	Units sold	Down arrow key
A13	Total Income	Down arrow key TWICE
A15	GRAND TOTAL	Down arrow key
A16	UNITS SOLD	Down arrow key TWICE
A18	Average Sale Price	Down arrow key
A19	Number of models	Down arrow ke
A20	Most sold	Down arrow ke
A21	Least sold	**Enter**
Click on D20	Rate of VAT	Down Arrow.

VAT is the acronym for Value Added Tax and is a percentage sales tax. A rate of 10% will mean 10% is to be added to the price. Such rates alter from time to time, so it will be important to allow for these changes in spreadsheets that use them.

Having typed all this in, it should be apparent that Column A is too tight and needs widening.

- Widen column A.

The chances are, at this stage, that you will not quite be able to see the whole of your spreadsheet. Quattro Pro has a maximise button that appears as an up arrow button in the top far right corner of the notebook area to the right of the notebook title. You will see that there are two small arrows, one pointing up and the other down. They are notebook maximise and minimise buttons. The maximise button points up and increases the size of the spreadsheet to take up the whole of the notebook area.

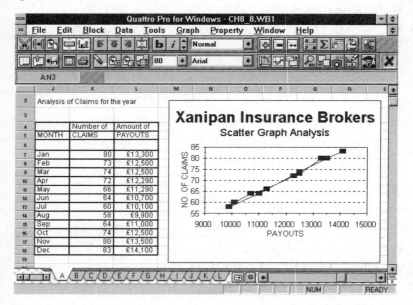

● Activate the maximise button with your mouse by placing the mouse pointer over it and clicking the left button on your mouse.

This should now leave you able to see more of your text. If you are a version 5.0 user, you may still find you are unable to see the bottom line of the active area of your spreadsheet. This can be put right by reducing the size of the scale of the spreadsheet. On the second speedbar appears a white box with the number in it. This number is a scaling factor set at 80%. Type in, say, 80 and you will see more of the spreadsheet.

—— 4.3 Good spreadsheet practice ——

Cell E20 will be used to store the current rate of VAT.

- Click on cell E20 and type in current rate of VAT as 17.5%. Including the percentage sign.

Quattro Pro will convert this percentage to a fraction but you will need to format the cell so that it is read as a percentage.

- Activate the notebook object inspector with your right-hand mouse button and select Numeric Format.

- From here click on Percent and accept the default number of decimal places as 2.

- Making sure that only cell E20 is highlighted, press **Enter** and the number should be presented as a decimal.

You will use this cell later to calculate the VAT to be charged on each car. This is good practice when designing a spreadsheet, as will be mentioned shortly.

- Type in the basic prices of the vehicles as whole numbers in cells B6 to F6.

The figures you are about to type in are currency, so you must change the Number Format to currency to 2 decimal places.

- Highlight cells B6 to F10

- Click on the highlighted area to activate the object inspector.

- Click on Number Format, then Currency and then OK.

- If the columns are too narrow, a row of ****** will warn you. Widen the cells as appropriate to allow all data to fit into the cells.

Now it is time to calculate the amount of VAT payable on the Net Price of each vehicle. Cell E20 is an absolute cell. For all vehicles, the VAT payable will be the price in the appropriate relative cell multiplied by the figure in the absolute cell E20. If the rate of VAT were to alter, you can simply type the new rate of VAT in cell E20 (not forgetting to include the % symbol) and the VAT amounts will automatically be recalculated in row 7. This is what was meant by adapting good spreadsheet practice.

- Click on cell B7, type in the formula +B6*$E$20 and press **Enter**.

Because the VAT cell is absolute, you can copy the formula to the rest of the vehicles and the VAT element will remain constant.

- With cell B7 highlighted, click on the Edit option, then Copy.

- Highlight cells C7 to F7, then click on the Edit option on the menu bar and then select Paste.

Examine each formula in cells B7 to F7 to appreciate how the concept of relative and absolute cell locations works. Also, try changing the rate of VAT, to appreciate what is happening.

- Click on cell B8 and type in the formula +B6+B7. This will add VAT to the basic price.

- Now copy the formula in cell B8 to the block C8 to F8.

Row 9 will contain a registration cost, which will be the same for all vehicles. It would again be good practice to use a single cell to reference this cost.

- Click on cell D19, type in Registration Cost and press **Enter**.

- Click on cell F19 and type in the number 100.

- Click on cell B9 and type in the formula +$F$19. Make this cell a currency format.

- Now Copy the formula in cell B9 to the block C9 to F9.

The formulae in the block of cells B9 to F9 contain only one single cell reference which has been fixed as absolute. You could just as easily have placed the number 100 into each cell. However, if the registration cost were to change, you would have six values to alter. Using this technique, you have only one cell to alter.

You can now arrive at the sale price.

- Click on cell B10 and enter the formula +B8+B9 to add the Registration Cost to the Gross Price.

- Copy the formula in cell B10 to the block C10 to F10.

As a final point to completing the top part of your spreadsheet, you should format remaining numbers as currency and to two places of decimals.

- Now type in the units sold on row 12 for each of the six vehicles.

- Click on cell B13 and type in the formula +B10*B12 to multiply the Sale Price with the Units Sold to give Total Income.

● Now Copy the formula in cell B13 to the block C13 to F13.

● Finally, format cells B13 to F13 as currency to 2 places of decimals.

The top part of your spreadsheet should now be complete. The next stages, before producing your first graph, will be to introduce you to a few new functions that you may well find useful in future.

———— 4.4 Some new functions ————

Cells B15 and B16 will contain the Total Income and Total Units sold, respectively. These will be calculated using the function SUM, which you have used before.

● Click on cell B15 and type in the function @SUM(B13..F13).

● Format this cell to currency and to zero decimal places so that the total is to the nearest whole £.

● Click on cell B16 and type in the function @SUM(B12..F12).

In cell B18 a function can be typed in that will calculate the average selling price based on the numbers in cells B10 to F10. Quattro Pro will add up the five prices and divide by five. The function that will do this automatically is AVG.

● Click on cell B18 and type in the function @AVG(B10..F10).

● Format this cell as currency, as before, this time to 2 decimal places.

Check with a calculator that this is correct.

Quattro Pro can also add up the number of cell entries in a block using the COUNT function.

In cell B19 you want to total the number of models in the Block B4 to F4. Although obvious at this stage, there may be an instance when you want to count entries in a much bigger block where some of the cells have no entries.

● Click on cell B19 and type in the function @COUNT(B4..F4).

Finally, in cells B20 and B21 you want the maximum and minimum numbers, respectively, in the block B12 to F12.

● Click on cell B20 and type in the function @MAX(B12..F12).

● Click on cell B21 and type in the function @MIN(B12..F12).

At the bottom of the spreadsheet, you have the page identification set as 'A'. For information this is not too helpful and it may be better to call the page 'January'.

● Point the mouse pointer at the tab A and click the right button of your mouse.

● Now type in January as your Page Name and click on OK.

● Finally, check that you are satisfied with the formats of all numbers, column widths, display style, and its accuracy before going any further.

——————— 4.5 Creating a bar chart ———————

What you will cover in this section is the production from the spreadsheet of a bar chart that shows the number of each vehicle type sold. All of the work in this section of the chapter will be carried out within the Graph pull-down menu.

● Click on the Graph option on the menu bar to pull down the graph options.

● Click on the New option.

This will reveal an object inspector. You will need to type in details about what is to be graphed.

You will notice that the new graph has been given the name Graph1. Although you can alter this, it is best to accept this graph name for now and go straight on to determining what has to be placed on the graph.

This is achieved by typing in the **Series range** details in the object inspector.

Deciding what to plot the figures against will be a matter of deciding what the X-Axis is to be. In this case the X-Axis will be the types of vehicles that are represented in the block of cells from B4 to F4.

What is needed next is to plot the number of units sold against each vehicle type. The first series will be the block of cell values showing the number sold for each vehicle: B12 to F12. For this chapter, this will be the only data plotted and so will be the only series.

● Type in as the X-Axis the block of cells from B4 to F4 by typing in B4..F4.

● Type in as the 1st Series the block of cells from B12 to F12 by typing in B12..F12.

Screen dump 4.2 shows the settings that should appear at this stage.

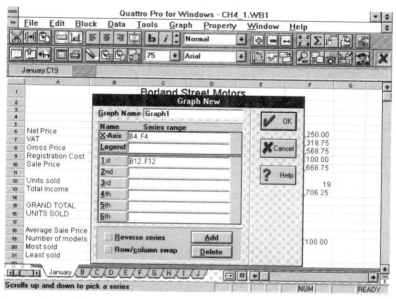

Screen dump 4.2

This now represents the bare minimum needed in order to create a graph.

● Click on OK at this point to see what kind of graph you have.

Screen dump 4.3 illustrates the graph you should have.

● If the graph mode does not occupy the whole spreadsheet, as it does in **Screen dump 4.3**, click on the graph maximise button that is placed to the right of the graph title.

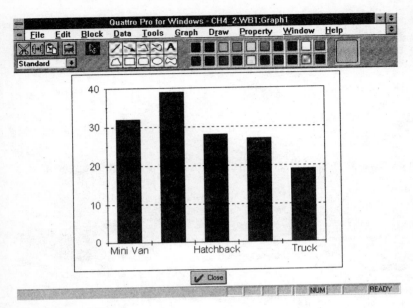

Screen dump 4.3

You have a problem in that not all the labels on the X Axis will be shown. This is simply because they take up too much room. You can, however, reduce the font size of the X-axis labels.

You will notice that the menu bar has changed slightly to give you a different set of options. This is to reflect the fact that you are in the Graph Editing mode and will require different utilities.

● Click on Property from the menu bar to pull down a new menu.

● From here click on X-Axis.

● Now click on the Text Font option and choose Point Size. Decrease the point size to 12 and then click on OK.

● Now return to your spreadsheet by clicking on the Close option at the foot of your graph.

● If you press function key **F11**, then click on Graph 1, you will see your graph full size.

The result should be similar to **Screen dump 4.4**

● Press the **Esc** key to return to the spreadsheet.

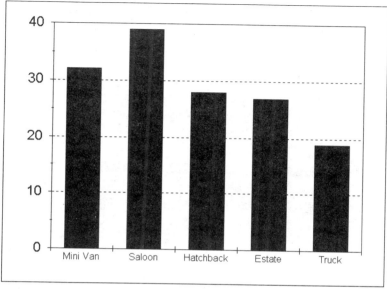

Screen dump 4.4

It was suggested earlier that if you change your data, in this case the number of units sold, then the graph would change to match the new data. Do this now and see the effect.

● Click on Graph from the menu bar, then Edit.

● Click on the Window option from the menu bar.

● Now Click on the Tile option.

This reveals both graph and spreadsheet in different windows. You can hop between the two windows using your mouse by placing clicking on the window you want to be in. The use of function key F6 does not work in the same way as it did before when you have a window that is a graph.

● Use your mouse to move between windows, observing what happens to the menu bar as you do so.

● Go back into your spreadsheet and change the figures in row 12 to the following:

Cell	Units sold
B12	51
C12	101

D12	14
E12	31
F12	62

You should be able to observe how the spreadsheet changes the graph as the numbers are altered. **Screen dump 4.5** shows the windowed effect. An obvious problem may be that you are unable to see clearly what is in each window because too much data and information now appears.

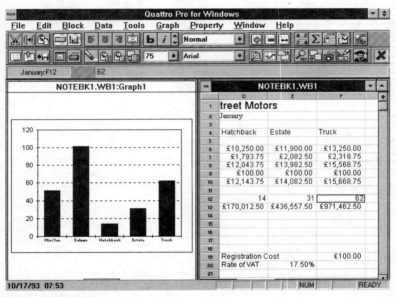

Screen dump 4.5

You could, of course, avoid the tiled windows and simply enter the new figures and press key F11. The use of function key F11 will by-pass the Graph menu and show you your newly drawn graph. When you press another key again, you will return to the spreadsheet at the point you left it.

At this stage, experiment a little with the numbers to see the effect.

● Expand the graph to fill the page so that you can more easily develop it. Remember, you can do this with your mouse by either clicking on the Maximise button, or dragging the edge of the graph window over the spreadsheet.

Although the graph is technically sound, you now need to add a few labels to the graph in order to give a better understanding as to what the graph is actually showing. At this stage the graph has no title and someone seeing such a graph for the first time would not know what the axes represent.

● Click on the Graph option from the menu bar, then click on Titles.

You now have an object inspector of blank lines to complete to give the graph a set of titles and, along with it, some real meaning.

● Type in the following titles:

Main Title	BORLAND STREET MOTORS
Subtitle	Sales for JANUARY
X Axis Title	Vehicle type
Y Axis Title	Number of units sold

And then click on OK to see the effect.

You will probably be left with a title that is too big. Once again, you will have to reduce the size of the font in the main heading.

● Place the mouse pointer over the title and click the left button of your mouse.

The effect of this is to make the title box the Object. Quattro Pro refers quite frequently to objects and you will have an opportunity to develop some sophisticated graphs using such objects in future chapters. For now, you will want to work on the object created by the graph facilities of Quattro Pro that has created your main title.

● Click on the Property option from the menu bar, then click on Current Object.

● This now reveals an object inspector, from which you should click on Text Font.

● Now click on Point Size and reduce it to 20.

● Click on OK to activate the change.

Screen dump 4.6 shows the graph with the appropriate titles and labels on the axis. This is now looking like a graph that could be presented to show what has happened with respect to the volume of sales.

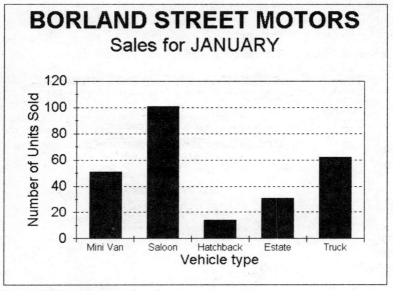

Screen dump 4.6

—— 4.6 Changing the graph type ——

Changing the graph is now simple.

● Click on the <u>G</u>raph option from the menu bar, then on Type.

● Now click on the small 3-D box to reveal a set of graph icons.

● Click on the pie chart.

● Now click on OK to activate the change.

The only problem you have with this is that the labels are again too large to fit on to your screen.

● Place the mouse pointer over the Pie and click the left button of your mouse.

This now makes the Pie the object.

● Click on the <u>P</u>roperty option on the menu bar, then on Current Object.

● This now reveals an object inspector, from which you should click on Text Fonts.

● Now click on Point Size and reduce it to 12.

● Now click on OK to activate the change.

Screen dump 4.7 Shows a resulting pie chart.

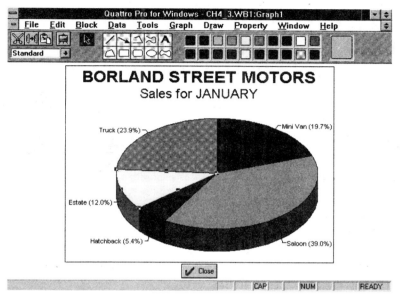

Screen dump 4.7

The pie chart is determined by the 1st series you selected earlier when determining the size of the bars in the bar chart. Each segment is a proportion of total sales, which Quattro Pro automatically calculates. You will also observe that Quattro Pro shows against each segment the actual units sold along with the percentage each represents of the whole volume. If you add these percentages together you get 100%.

In the case of both graph types, Quattro Pro also determines the scale of each so that it fills up a reasonable proportion of the screen. Such control of your graph can be over-ridden by you, which will be left as a topic for Chapter 8.

This data can also be shown effectively as a COLUMN graph.

● Click on Graph, then Type.

● Now click on 3D, then on Column, which is represented as a single multi-coloured three-dimensional bar.

● Now click on OK to view the graph.

This is not a lot different from the pie chart, as it shows how the total number of units has been split up between the vehicle types.

—————— 4.7 Printing your graph ——————

In most cases this should prove quite straightforward. In order to print a graph, you will need to have a graphics printer. Nearly all matrix, ink-jet and laser printers are capable of printing graphics.

● Make sure there is paper in your printer and the printer is switched on.

● Make sure you are in the graph edit mode so that the computer can recognise that it is a graph you want printed and not your spreadsheet.

● Click on File, then Page Preview so that you can have a look at what the printed output will look like.

On the screen should appear a small icon of the outline of a magnifying glass. This is a zoom icon and allows you a closer look at the page you are previewing. You can move this icon with your mouse.

● Move the magnifying glass icon somewhere on the chart and click your left mouse button.

Screen dump 4.8 shows the 200% magnification that should have been achieved.

At the top of the screen is a small print icon. This allows you to start printing your graph and will return the screen to the spreadsheet.

● Click on the print icon to start printing.

An alternative would have been to select Print from the File pull-down menu and to begin printing the graph without previewing it.

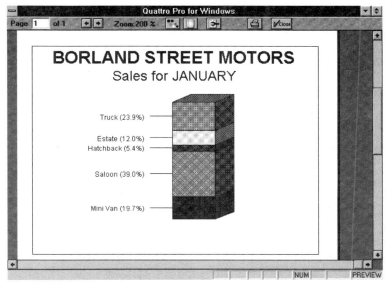

Screen dump 4.8

— 4.8 Inserting your graph into your — spreadsheet

In the final section of this chapter, you will place your graph into your spreadsheet. Up to now, you can see either your graph or your spreadsheet, or both using the Tile option.

First make a convenient space on the spreadsheet and then insert the graph into it. From here on you can make alterations and see, at a glance the impact it will have on the spreadsheet.

The graph you have produced will, for the purpose of this exercise, be placed in the block of cells C14 to E26. If you observe your spreadsheet so far, you will see that the Registration details and VAT rate have been placed in this block. Begin by moving them out of the way first.

● Highlight cells D19 to E20.

● Click on Edit, then Cut.

This places the block of cells into the Clipboard and removes it, temporarily, from the spreadsheet.

● Click on A22 to move the cell pointer to indicate the destination.

● Click on the Edit, then Paste.

You will observe that at this stage the cell content of the VAT has preserved its percentage format. More importantly, all the cells that used the VAT rate in E20 to calculate the actual amount of VAT have adjusted their formulae to alter to where the VAT rate has now been moved. Consequently, the effect of moving such a cell has been right across the spreadsheet.

This now leaves you with the space for your graph.

The next stage is to insert the graph into this part of the spreadsheet.

● Click on Graph, then Insert.

● You will be asked which graph to insert. At this stage you only have Graph1. Click on this one.

● A small graph icon appears which is controlled with your mouse. Press the left-hand mouse button and drag the pointer to produce a rectangle on the spreadsheet. When you let go of the button the graph will fill the space you outlined.

● From the Graph pull-down menu select Type and choose, from the 2-D section, the pie chart.

The graph is changed instantly and appears on the spreadsheet as shown in **Screen dump 4.9**.

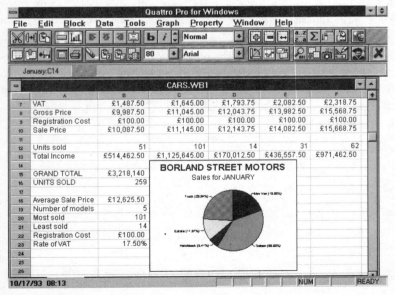

Screen dump 4.9

● Click on a cell in row 12 and alter each number of vehicles sold.

As you change the data, you should observe the instant effect it has on the graph.

This entire spreadsheet, with graph, can now be printed in exactly the same way as you printed the spreadsheet before.

● Experiment with this by altering both the number of cars sold and the type of graph you want to see.

● Save the file as CARS when you have the latest version you are satisfied with.

● Now print the entire spreadsheet.

—— 4.9 Reading the indicator ——

In the bottom right-hand corner of your screen, on the status line, appears a piece of information that tells you something about the status of your spreadsheet. This mode indicator changes as you perform different functions. Here are the most common indicators:

Indicator	Mode
EDIT	You pressed F2 (EDIT) to edit an entry; you are entering or editing text in a text box; or you made an incorrect entry
ERROR	Quattro Pro is displaying a message. Choose Help or press F1 (HELP) to get Help; Select OK to clear the message.
LABEL	You are entering a label.
MENU	You clicked the menu bar, or pressed the Alt or F10 (MENU); or you are in an object inspector with Quattro Pro waiting for input.
POINT	You are specifying a block before choosing a command, while working in an object inspector, or entering a formula.
READY	Quattro Pro is ready for you to enter or choose a command.

VALUE   You are entering a value.

WAIT   Quattro Pro is completing a command or process, such as saving a file.

Refer to the mode indicator if you get stuck.

——— 4.10 Chapter summary ———

In this chapter you have concentrated on some of the many statistical functions and formulae available in Quattro Pro and utilised a few of the graph formats available. In particular you have:

● Covered more work on text, values, formulae and function entries to cells.

● Altered the style and presentation of the spreadsheet.

● Copied blocks of cells with absolute and relative formula contents.

● Produced a graph.

● Labelled the graph with text.

● Generated different graphs.

● Printed the graph.

● Inserted the graph in the spreadsheet.

5

STYLE AND PRESENTATION

5.1 Aims of this chapter

This chapter concentrates on a number of issues regarding the set-up of your spreadsheet and how to present your data in a form that is appropriate to the problem in hand. It will also explain the good practice of naming areas of your spreadsheet.

The first part of the chapter is based around a stock system set out in tabular form showing data in a number of different formats.

The second part of the chapter is based on a sales report showing sales and profit figures in a simple table with a chart and a significant amount of text. The text will be manipulated in a way similar a word processor.

5.2 Formatting numbers

As a starting-point examine the spreadsheet in **Screen dump 5.1,** which lists items of stock showing Stock Code, Description, Quantity in stock, Cost Price, and Selling Price. Note that the scale of the spreadsheet has been reduced to 70%. This was needed for Version 5.0 so that the whole of the active spreadsheet became visible.

- In order to get started, type in the data in **Screen dump 5.1** in a new spreadsheet.

- If you have not already done so, widen column B.

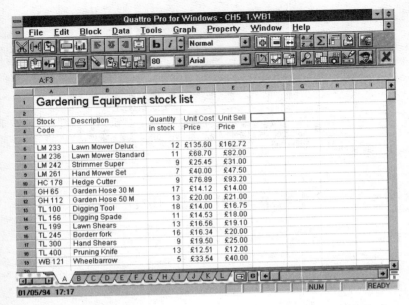

Screen dump 5.1

- The heading has been given a larger font. To achieve this, activate the notebook object inspector using the right button on your mouse while you have the pointer in the notebook area. (For version 5.0 you will need to click on the object properties option from a list of options.)

- Click on the Font option.

From here you can increase the point size to 18, which is the size of the one that appears in **Screen dump 5.1**.

- The numbers in columns D and E are currency. Highlight the cells and the activate the notebook object inspector again and click on Numeric Format from the object properties.

- Now click on the currency option and set them to 2 places of decimal.

Finally, you should set the currency symbol as £.

- Place the mouse pointer at the top of the screen over the title bar and click the right hand button of your mouse.

- Now click on the International option and from here click on Currency.

- Set currency to £ and prefixed.

—————— 5.3 Date formats ——————

In this and the next section, you will examine in more detail some of the other formats available in Quattro Pro. You now have enough information to type in to the spreadsheet stock details about value and possible profit.

● Click on cell F3 and type in the label Stock and then type in the label Value in cell F4.

● Now click on cell F6 and type in the formula +C6*D6.

The formula in cell F6 multiplies Stock Quantity with Cost Price. Do not copy this formula yet, as you will do that later.

● Click on cell G3 and type in the label Unit and type in the label Profit in cell G4.

● Now click on cell G6 and type in the formula +E6–D6.

The formula in cell G6 subtracts Cost Price from Selling Price to give the Unit Profit. Again, do not copy this formula yet.

● Click On cell H3 and type in the label Gross and in cell H4 type in the label Profit.

● Now click on cell H6 and type in the formula +C6*G6.

The formula in cell H6 multiplies the Stock Quantity with the Unit Profit to give the Gross Profit per line.

● Format the block F6 to H6 as currency, to 2 decimal places.

● Widen column F to reveal all data.

At this stage, you now have three formulae that can be copied down the spreadsheet in one operation.

● Highlight the cells F6 to H6.

● Click on the Edit option from the menu bar and, from the pull-down menu, click on Copy to place a copy of the formulae in the clipboard.

● Now highlight the destination cells F7 to H19.

● Click on Edit from the menu bar and then click on Paste.

Notice how the formats have also copied through.

● Click on cell E10, type in 72, and observe how the Unit Profit appears as a negative to indicate a loss and how the formats have remained as currency.

	A	B	C	D	E	F	G	H
1	Gardening Equipment stock list							
2								
3	Stock	Description	Quantity	Unit Cost	Unit Sell	Stock	Unit	Gross
4	Code		in stock	Price	Price	Value	Profit	Profit
5								
6	LM 233	Lawn Mower Delux	12	£135.60	£162.72	£1,627.20	£27.12	£325.44
7	LM 236	Lawn Mower Standard	11	£68.70	£82.00	£755.70	£13.30	£146.30
8	LM 242	Strimmer Super	9	£25.45	£31.00	£229.05	£5.55	£49.95
9	LM 261	Hand Mower Set	7	£40.00	£47.50	£280.00	£7.50	£52.50
10	HC 178	Hedge Cutter	9	£76.89	£72.00	£692.01	(£4.89)	(£44.01)
11	GH 65	Garden Hose 30 M	17	£14.12	£14.00	£240.04	(£0.12)	(£2.04)
12	GH 112	Garden Hose 50 M	13	£20.00	£21.00	£260.00	£1.00	£13.00
13	TL 100	Digging Tool	18	£14.00	£16.75	£252.00	£2.75	£49.50
14	TL 156	Digging Spade	11	£14.53	£18.00	£159.83	£3.47	£38.17
15	TL 199	Lawn Shears	13	£16.56	£19.10	£215.28	£2.54	£33.02
16	TL 245	Borderr fork	16	£16.34	£20.00	£261.44	£3.66	£58.56
17	TL 300	Hand Shears	9	£19.50	£25.00	£175.50	£5.50	£49.50
18	TL 400	Pruning Knife	13	£12.51	£12.00	£162.63	(£0.51)	(£6.63)
19	WB 121	Wheelbarrow	5	£33.54	£40.00	£167.70	£6.46	£32.30

Screen dump 5.2

At this stage your spreadsheet should be fairly full and looking similar to **Screen dump 5.2**. The next stage is to type in a date when the stock was received. You will also create a column to store the number of days the stock has been held. In doing this, you will learn a little about the Quattro Pro date function and how it can be used.

The date in the date function appears in the format @DATE(94,6,22) where:

94 is the year 1994

6 is the month 6 or June

22 is the day in the month

You are able to type in a date into a cell but will not see it appear in an immediately recognisable format, as you will now find out.

● Click on cell I3 and type in the label Last and in cell I4 type in the label Delivery.

● Now click on cell I6 and type in the date function
@DATE(94,05,20).

What will appear in the cell is the number 34474. This is the
number of days between 1 January 1900 and what was typed in (20
May 1994). This may seem odd at first, but this will allow you to
perform some useful calculations. However, to make sense of it you
will need to alter its format.

● Highlight the whole block where the dates are to appear; i.e.
cells I6 to I19.

● With the mouse pointer on the block, click on the right mouse
button to activate the notebook object inspector.

● Click on the Numeric Format from the box properties, and from
here click on the Date option.

● From the date formats available, click on the one that appears as
DD-MMM-YY.

● Click on OK.

● Widen column I to reveal the date formats.

Although only the one cell has an actual date in it, Quattro Pro
allows you to prepare in advance the cell format for future input.

● Type in the following dates in their respective cells.

Cell	Date
I7	@DATE(94,5,19)
I8	@DATE(94,6,23)
I9	@DATE(94,6,29)
I10	@DATE(94,6,01)
I11	@DATE(94,6,02)
I12	@DATE(94,6,12)
I13	@DATE(94,6,12)
I14	@DATE(94,5,30)
I15	@DATE(94,6,12)
I16	@DATE(94,5,29)
I17	@DATE(94,6,05)

I18	@DATE(94,6,06)
I19	@DATE(94,6,10)

As you type in these dates you should see the requested format appear. Column J will hold the number of days between the date of the last delivery and the current date. What you need, therefore, is a facility where the computer can calculate this for you. The function that does this is @TODAY.

● Click on cell A21 and type in the label Date.

● Now click on cell B21 and type in @TODAY.

● Format the date in cell B21 as you did before using the date DD-MMM-YY.

Providing your computer has the correct date and time set, you should see today's date showing. If the date is wrong, then type in today's date in the cell using the date function. The benefit of the TODAY function over DATE is that if you return to the spreadsheet on another day, the date is altered automatically.

You now have the facility to show the days lapsed between a delivery and today for each item of stock.

● Click on cell J3 and type in the label Days and in J4 type in the label Lapsed.

● Click on cell J6 and type in the formula +$B$21–I6.

This calculates the number of days from today to the date of the last delivery. Notice also how the cell location B21 in the formula has been set as an absolute.

● Now copy the formula in cell J6 to the block J7 to J14.

─────────── **5.4 Naming blocks** ───────────

This section will show you how you can give a block of cells a distinct name rather than identifying it by its cells. The purpose of this is that it is very much easier to remember the name of a block rather than the co-ordinates of a block. It will also serve as a useful way of documenting what is on your spreadsheet.

- Highlight cells F6 to F19.

- Click on <u>B</u>lock from the menu bar and then click on the <u>N</u>ames option.

- Now click on the <u>C</u>reate option and give it the block <u>N</u>ame Stock Value.

- Now click on cell F21 and type in the formula that will calculate the sum: @SUM(Stock Value). Format the cell to currency.

Instead of using the block cells references in the formula, you were able to use the block name. This will make the spreadsheet much easier to follow if you want to return to it at a later stage and examine the formulae.

- Highlight cells G6 to G19.

- Click on <u>B</u>lock from the menu bar and then click on the <u>N</u>ames option.

- Now click on the <u>C</u>reate option and give it the block <u>N</u>ame Unit Profit.

You will notice that next to the <u>C</u>reate option in the pull-down menu is Ctrl+F3. This means that you are able to activate Create by holding down the **Control** key and pressing the function key **F3** once, instead of using the pull-down menu.

- Highlight the block H6 to H19.

- Holding down the Control key, press the function key F3 once and give the block the name Gross Profit.

- Now click on cell H21 and type in the formula to calculate the sum: @SUM(Gross Profit).

- Highlight cells J6 to J19.

- Give the block the name Days Lapsed.

You now have a collection of these block names and it is always a good idea to keep a list of them somewhere. Fortunately, Quattro Pro will do this for you.

- Click on the Block option from the menu bar and then click on Names again.

- Now click the <u>M</u>ake Table option.

This will create a table of blocks with names for you and Quattro Pro now needs to know where to put them.

● Type in the cell location as B24 and click on OK.

● Now go to cell B24 to see the effect.

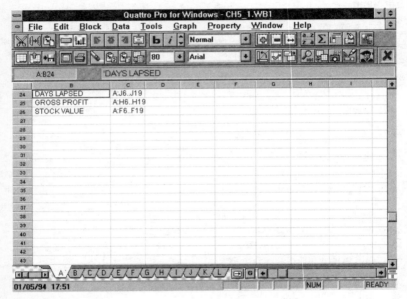

Screen dump 5.3

Screen dump 5.3 shows the table. As a final illustration of their use, do the following.

● Click on cell E22, type in the label Average Unit Profit, then type in cell G22 the function @AVG(Unit Profit).

● Click on cell H22 and type in the label Average Days Lapsed and type in cell J22 the function @AVG(Days Lapsed).

● Using the Numeric Format from the notebook object inspector, set up the following formats:

 F21, G22, H21 to Currency and to two decimal places

 J22 as fixed to 1 place of decimals.

Not only will it be easier to identify how formulae are made up, it also reads better.

—— 5.5 Summarising the formats ——

In the notebook object inspector, you have now explored most Numeric Format settings. This section simply starts by summarising them as a way of covering the section of the menu system available.

To format a block of cells you first have to highlight the range with your mouse and then activate the notebook object inspector with the right button of your mouse. An alternative way is to highlight the block and then click on the Current Object option from the Property pull-down menu.

The formats are:

Fixed
: Displays numbers to a specified number of decimal places, a minus for negatives, and a leading zero for decimal values.

Scientific
: Numbers are displayed in the form of e.g. 4.733E–2. This scientific form is similar to that available on most calculators.

Currency
: Currency symbols are used as prefixes or suffixes, depending how you have determined them. Thousands are separated with commas. Negative numbers can be bracketed.

Comma
: Commas are used to separate thousands. Negative numbers can be bracketed.

General
: The default format. Numbers are displayed with a minus sign for negatives, no thousands separators, and no trailing zeros to the right of the decimal point.

+/-
: This converts numbers to rows of + (plus) or – (minus). The number 5 would be displayed as +++++ while – 3 would appear as – – –

Percent
: This multiplies a stored number by 100, sets it to a specified number of decimal places and places a % sign after it.

Date
: As shown in this chapter, converts a number to a specified date format.

Time   Changes the time format.

Text   This displays the cell formulae rather than in their
                    computed values.

Hidden   This allows you to hide cell contents from display
                    without actually removing them from the spread-
                    sheet.

User Defined   This lets you choose from a list of formats formerly
                    created from customising your own formats.

Alignment settings are also available from the notebook object
inspector.

General   This restores text and numbers so that text is left-
                    justified and numbers are right-justified.

Left   This left-justifies all data in cells.

Right   This right-justifies all data in cells.

Center   This centres all data in cells.

● Highlight the block of cells where the headings are, A3 to J4,
  and centre-align the labels.

── 5.6 Protecting blocks of cells ──

This final section that deals with your current spreadsheet, will
show you how to protect blocks of cells from being overwritten.
The technique requires you to:

1 Protect the whole page from being written on.

2 Unprotect those blocks of cells that you want the user to type in
   data to.

In this case, you will name the block of cells containing the stock
codes and their description and then protect it from a user overwrit-
ing the cells.

● Place your mouse pointer at the page indicator 'A' which is at
  the bottom of the notebook area.

● Now click the right mouse button to reveal the Active Page
  inspector.

- Click on Protection.
- Click on the Enable option.

The whole spreadsheet is now protected which means you cannot type data into any of the cells.

- Try to alter one of the figures or labels and see what happens.

Now you need to *unprotect* those cells where you want data typed in. There are two such blocks. The first is block C6 to E19 containing Quantity in Stock, Unit Cost, and Selling Price, and the block I6 to I19 containing Last Delivery Date.

- Highlight the block C6 to E19.
- Click the right mouse button to reveal the Active Page inspector.
- Click on Unprotect.
- Repeat this for the block I6 to I19.

This leaves all the cells with formulae and labels as protected, while the other cells can have their data altered. It might now be worth your while trying to type data into the protected cells and then typing in data in those cells where you are allowed to type in data to confirm that you have the desired outcome.

Disabling Protect from the Active Page inspector will remove all protection settings.

——————— 5.7 Presenting text ———————

The second part of this chapter deals with text in more detail and some of the presentation qualities available in the Quattro Pro package. The concentration is very much on visual appearance. In a new spreadsheet, you will type in details concerning an improvement in sales performance. The spreadsheet will have a distinct number of sections to it: a heading, a boxed article of text, a table, and a floating graph.

First, the heading:

- In cell A1 type Bumper Sales and Profits for the year.

● Now use the Font option from the notebook object inspector to enhance the heading.

Typing in the text which follows will prove a little more interesting. You will type the text in just two cells to start with and then get Quattro Pro to rearrange it in a different block of cells. Observe what appears in **Screen dump 5.4.**

The text typed into cell A3 is much longer than can appear on one line and appears to go off the screen. You can type up to 256 characters in a single line.

● Type the following text in cell A3 remembering NOT to press the Enter key:

As shown in the graph, we are pleased to report a significant increase in our sales for the last year. As you can see from the graph, sales are up and, in addition to this, we are pleased to report that this has resulted in a corresponding rise in ● profits. Type the following in cell A4: We are also pleased to report that this rise over the last year is expected to continue into next year even and into the foreseeable future.

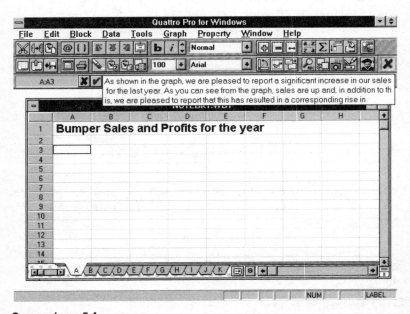

Screen dump 5.4

You will now ask Quattro Pro to take this text and reformat it into a block of cells, making all text visible.

● Click on <u>B</u>lock from the menu bar and then click on the <u>R</u>eformat option.

You are now being asked to define both where the block is and where it is to be formatted.

● Highlight cells A3 to D15 and press the **Enter** key.

The text will now have been reformatted into this block. This will allow you to have columns of text similar to that of newspapers.

——— 5.8 Search and replace text ———

If you use a word processing package, then you will already be familiar with this facility. Quattro Pro can scan through a block of text searching for a word (or string of characters) and replace it. As an example you will scan through the text to replace 'report' with 'announce'.

● Highlight cells A3 to D15.

● Click on <u>B</u>lock from the menu bar and then click on <u>N</u>ames.

● Now click on <u>C</u>reate, and <u>N</u>ame the block ARTICLE.

This names that part of the spreadsheet where the text is stored so that it can be referenced much more easily in future.

● Click on Edit from the menu bar, then click on Search and Replace.

● In the <u>B</u>lock(s) box, type in the block name ARTICLE.

Although the block name appears in upper case here, it does not matter if you use lower case or a mixture of both. This applies to any use of a block name in these instances.

● In the <u>F</u>ind box type in report.

● In the <u>R</u>eplace box type in announce.

At this point you should have a screen similar to that shown in **Screen dump 5.5** which shows the settings made.

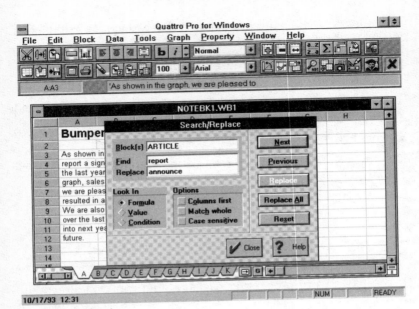

Screen dump 5.5

The Look in panel determines which aspect of a formula Quattro Pro is to look at when replacing, whether it is to look into the formula itself or at the values the formulae place in the cell. As you are replacing text, the setting of this is irrelevant.

There are three option settings:

Columns first will determine the direction of the search: one column after the other rather than one row after the other. Leaving this blank, the search starts at row 3 and works down to row 15.

Match whole will search for the word 'report' as a whole word only.

Case sensitive reads 'Report' and 'report' differently.

The right-hand part of the object inspector will start a number of activities working:

The Next option will find the next appearance of the word 'report' in the text, while Previous will go backwards through the process.

Replace will replace the next occurrence of the word.

Replace <u>A</u>ll will perform the search and replace through all the text in the named block.

Re<u>s</u>et clears the settings in the object inspector.

● Click on the Replace <u>A</u>ll option.

● Now go through the article correcting any anomalies that may have occurred. For example, 'reporting' has been replaced with 'announceing' (instead of 'announcing').

——— 5.9 Inserting graphs into a ——— spreadsheet

● Take a look at **Screen dump 5.6** to see what is to be achieved.

Screen dump 5.6 is a print preview of the final spreadsheet and has been magnified to 200% using the zoom facility shown to you in Chapter 4.

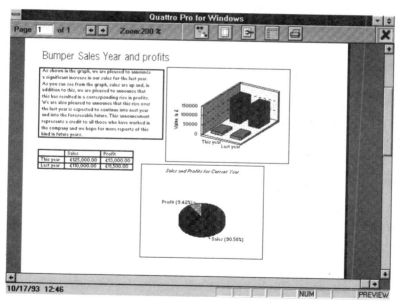

Screen dump 5.6

● Type in the table that appears to the left of the screen dump.

Cell	Data
A17	This year
A18	Last year
B16	Sales
C16	Profit
B17	125,000
B18	110,000
C17	13,000
C18	11,500

● Format the four numeric values to currency with zero decimal places.

● If necessary, widen columns B and C so that the numbers will show.

● Highlight cells A3 to D14 and, from the block notebook object inspector, click on the Line Drawing option.

● Click on Outline and then click on the thick line option followed by clicking on OK.

● Click on the Block option from the menu bar, then on Reformat and type in the block reference as ARTICLE.

The purpose of using Reformat again is to take advantage of the wider columns.

● Widen column D so that the thick border line is not obscuring any of the text.

● Now highlight the table from cell A16 to C18 and, from the block notebook object inspector, give the block thick lines around all cells.

At this stage you now have the text and tables all nicely boxed up. The next stage will be to create two graphs based on the data in the table. From here, you will insert them into the spreadsheet.

The first graph will plot in 3-D bar chart form both the sales and profit for each of the two years; this year and last.

● Click on the Graph option from the menu bar and then click on New.

● Accept the suggested graph name as Graph1 and type in the following three series:

X-Axis	A17..A18	(year labels)
1st	B17..B18	(sales figures)
2nd	C17..C18	(profit figures)

Then click on OK. A bar graph will appear.

● From the Graph menu click on the Type option.

● Click on 3-D Bar option.

● From the Graph menu click on Titles and type in the Y1-Axis Title as:

Value in £.

You will see from the resulting graph that there is no real need for a title as it is largely self evident as to what the bars represent. Also, as the graph is to appear in the spreadsheet itself, there is no need to give it a main title.

Before moving on to the next graph, you will have the opportunity to examine another object inspector by activating it with your mouse.

● Making sure the mouse pointer is in the graph, click the right button on your mouse to activate the general graph object inspector.

● Click on Graph Setup and Background Properties

● Now click on Box Type to see the options available.

● Make it a 3-D box.

Your graph does not have to have a box around at all and this is an option in the list of boxes.

The default box is a thin line.

● Check that this is the graph required and then return to the spreadsheet by clicking on the spreadsheet name from the Window pull-down menu.

You now have your first graph created and named. Quattro Pro allows you create other graphs in the current spreadsheet provided they have different names.

- From the <u>G</u>raph pull-menu click on <u>N</u>ew again and accept the suggested graph name Graph2.

- Type in the two series in turn:

  <u>X</u>-Axis   B16..C16 (year labels)

  <u>1</u>st   B17..C17 (sales and profit figures)

Then click on OK. A bar graph will appear.

- From the Graph menu click on the <u>T</u>ype option.

- Click on 3-D Pie option.

With the mouse pointer in the graph, click the right-hand mouse button and choose Graph Titles. As <u>M</u>ain Title type in Sales and Profit for Current Year, then click on OK.

You will notice that the title is too big to fit the graph box. You will now need to reduce the font size by activating, with your mouse, another object inspector.

- With your mouse pointer over the heading of the pie chart, click the left button.

The small boxes around the title indicate that the title is now the object. This can now be used to activate a new object inspector specific to this object.

- Use your mouse to activate the object inspector.

- Now click on Text Font, set the point size to 18, and set it in <u>B</u>old and <u>I</u>talics.

- Check that this is the graph you want and return to the spreadsheet.

- Now return to your spreadsheet.

In this final section of this chapter, you will insert the two graphs into your spreadsheet and learn how to move them, your text and table around the spreadsheet.

- Click on <u>G</u>raph, then on <u>I</u>nsert.

- Now click on Graph1, then on OK.

At this stage a small graph icon appears that can be moved with your mouse. This allows you to decide on where you want it placed on your spreadsheet.

● Move the icon to cell F3 and click the left button.

The graph now appears on the spreadsheet as an object and will be off the screen. Before moving the graphs around the spreadsheet it is worth placing the other one on the spreadsheet.

● Insert Graph2 at cell F14 in the same way as you did Graph1.

Now to move the graph around. First you must identify the graph as an object and then, with your mouse, move the object around. If you are familiar with Windows applications you will know how to do this.

● Place the pointer over the first graph and click the left button of your mouse.

A few small boxes should now appear around the graph to indicate it is now the object you are to work with.

● Now press the LEFT button of your mouse and keep it pressed. A small hand will appear over the graph.

● Keeping the mouse button depressed, move the mouse slowly and you will see the object move as well.

● Position the graph where you wish it and let go of the mouse button to confirm the new location.

● Repeat this for the second graph.

You can also move blocks of cells around the spreadsheet in exactly the same way.

● Highlight the cells that contain your data table making sure you also include the lines.

At this stage make sure the block is highlighted in black.

● Position the mouse pointer over the highlighted block and hold the left mouse button down.

● Keeping the mouse button depressed, move the mouse slowly and you will see the block of cells move.

● Position the table where you wish and let go of the mouse button to confirm the new location, being careful not to place the table over the article.

The block of cells can be moved in the same way as a graphics object. However, the graph can be placed over blocks of cells without you losing any data. The cell contents can be hidden behind the graph and revealed by your moving the graph later. Quattro Pro refers to such objects as floating objects. However, if you move blocks of data around, they actually occupy the cells themselves. You will be warned by Quattro Pro if such a movement is likely to result in any loss of data.

- Now make sure your mouse pointer is somewhere on the spreadsheet and not over a graph.

- Click on the File option on the menu bar and then click on Page Preview to see what your printed output would look like.

- Print your spreadsheet.

- Now alter the numbers in the data table to see the effect it has on the two graphs that have been inserted into your spreadsheet.

- Now save your file with the name ARTICLE.

—————— 5.10 Chapter summary ——————

It is worth noting that spreadsheets are often set up by people who gained an expertise in this area but are operated by others who simply want to look at the data and carry out simple operations. Good presentation is very important if someone without great skills in spreadsheet handling needs to extract information from them. In addition, you may find yourself returning to spreadsheets you have designed after a long absence. The situation can easily arise where you cannot find your way around your own spreadsheet if it is badly presented and muddled. Therefore, presentation and organisation, a central theme of this chapter, are important to consider carefully.

In this chapter you have:

- Altered cell widths to fit the data in them.

- Named and used blocks as both a way of better documentation and a more efficient way of working with blocks.

- Had more practice with formatting blocks of cells.

- Altered the displayed currency symbols.

- Used the Quattro Pro date function for display and calculations.

- Protected blocks of data from being over written.

- Written and manipulated text boxes.

- Used search and replace.

- Created different kinds graphs.

- Inserted graphs into a spreadsheet.

- Moved graphs, as objects, around the spreadsheet.

- Moved highlighted blocks, as objects, around the spreadsheet.

- Produced attractively presented text, data and graphs.

6

DATES AND DECISIONS

6.1 Aims of this chapter

This chapter further develops the use of dates, building up formulae and moving blocks of cell contents around the spreadsheet. The chapter also looks at Quattro Pro's ability to ask questions and give results based on these questions. The chapter does this with two examples: trading in shares and a monthly sales analysis.

6.2 More practice with formats

This first example is designed to show you more about writing formulae, manipulating dates, moving blocks and inserting rows and columns.

Screen dump 6.3 is what you are aiming for (note the three parts). You will set it up in a slightly different way across the screen so that you can move things around for practice.

- Start with a blank spreadsheet and type in a company title – Windows Savings Trust will do but use any company name you wish.

- Next type in some identification labels. Use your mouse to speed things up.

In cell	type
D3	Commission rate
A4	Purchase
A6	date
B6	shares
C6	price
D6	commission
E6	cost

● Widen column D so that the entire word Commission is visible by placing the cell pointer at the top right of column heading D and, holding your right mouse button down, dragging it wider.

● Type in cell F3 the value 3%. The number 0.03 will appear in the control panel; 3% in the spreadsheet when formatted.

● Now format cell F3 using the Numeric Format option from the Block notebook object inspector. You want the Percent option from this and to format it to one decimal place.

● Centre the labels in cells A6 to E6.

● Highlight cells A5 to E5.

● Place the mouse pointer over the highlighted block and right click your mouse.

● From the block properties option click Shading to reveal an object inspector containing two palettes of colours.

You can click on a colour from each palette to create a different blend of colours in the Blend panel below.

● Click on two darker colours and observe how the Blends alter.

● Using the Blend panel, click on a dark shade and then click on OK.

● Repeat this operation for the shaded block that appears in row 7 from A7 to E7.

● Use the Font selection from the Block notebook object inspector to enlarge the headings point size in cell A1.

At this stage you should have a spreadsheet looking similar to that in **Screen dump 6.1**.

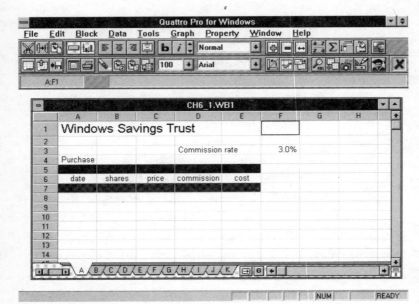

Screen dump 6.1

— 6.3 More on manipulating dates —

Begin by typing the purchase date, 20 October, 1989. You could type in the date as a label by prefixing it with an apostrophe. However, in this exercise, you will want the computer to perform some arithmetic on this date which will require the entry to be typed in as a function similar to that performed in Chapter 5.

● Click on cell A8 and type in @DATE(89,10,20), that is Year, Month, Day.

The figure 32801 should appear which, remember, represents the number of days since 1 January 1900. At this stage it would be wise to format this number so that it displays a date of some meaning.

● Highlight cells A8 to A10 to indicate that you want three cells formatted for dates.

● From the Block notebook object inspector click on the Numeric Format option. Click on the Date function and, from this, click on the Date Format DD-MMM-YY (Day-Month-Year), as shown in **Screen dump 6.2**.

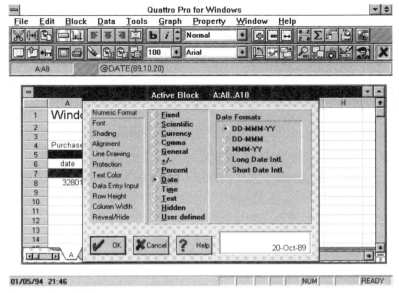

Screen dump 6.2

Remember, Quattro Pro allows you to format cells before you type in data.

- Widen column A so that the formatted dates are revealed.

- Type in 100 in cell B8, which will be the number of shares purchased.

- Type in the share price in cell C8 as 0.5 (50 pence).

- Now format the block C8 to E10 as currency and to two decimal places.

You may also need to set the currency to £ using the International option from the Application object inspector that can be activated by pressing your right mouse button with the pointer on the title bar.

- Click on cell D8 and type in the formula +B8*C8*$F$3.

The formula in cell D8 contains an absolute cell reference F3. Remember, when this formula is copied, all cell references with a dollar sign placed in front of them will not alter while others will change relative to the cell they are copied to.

You will see the figure £1.50 in D8.

● Click on cell E8, type in the formula +B8*C8+D8.

The formula in cell E8 multiplies the number of shares by the price per share and then adds the commission to this to give the final cost of this transaction.

● Now type in the next two rows of data:

In cell	type
A9	The@DATE for 17 February 1991
B9	The number 500
C9	The number 1.5 (this will appear as £1.50)
A10	The @DATE for 18 August 1993
B10	The number 150
C10	The number 1 (this will appear as £1.00)

● Now copy the formulae in the source cells D8 to E8 to the destination cells D9 to E10.

● Save the spreadsheet with the name HST1.

Regular saving of your work at intervals is recommended. Situations do arise when you are drawn away from your computer

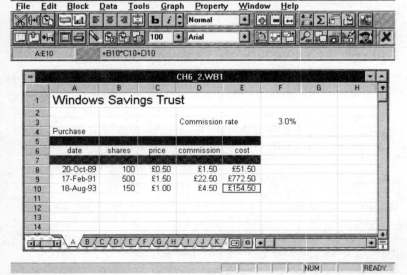

Screen dump 6.3

and the system is shut down by someone else, leaving all your efforts as lost. You may also experience power failures or make a silly mistake that causes your work to be lost. Saving your work every, say, 30 minutes means that, at worst, you need only go back 30 minutes if your spreadsheet is inadvertently lost.

At this stage you should have a spreadsheet similar to that shown in **Screen dump 6.3.**

—— 6.4 Copying blocks of cells ——

In this section we will expand the spreadsheet to include details about the sale of the shares. As the sales information will be similar to the purchase, it seems common sense to take advantage of the fact.

● Highlight cells A4 to E10.

● Click on the Block option on the menu bar and then click on the Names option followed by Create.

● Type in Purchase.

● Now click on the Copy command from the Block pull-down menu and type in the source block name Purchase. This will copy the contents of the block to the Clipboard.

● Now click on cell F4 and then click on the Paste option from the Edit full down menu.

● Widen both columns F and I to 11 characters. You will need to do each column separately.

Take note now of how Quattro Pro has copied the block. It assumes that F4 is the top left cell of the block copied in the same way as A4 is of the source block. In order to be consistent in naming blocks, it should be done for this next block.

● Highlight cells F4 to J10.

● Click on the Names option from the Block pull-down menu.

● From here, click on Create and type in a name for the block as Sale.

(For the time being, the entire spreadsheet will not be visible on the screen and the block Sale will still have the on-screen label Purchase.)As a further demonstration of the benefits of naming blocks try the following.

● Go to cell A1 by pressing the **Home** key on the keyboard.

● Now press function key F5, which is the 'go to' key.

● Instead of typing a cell reference, type in Sale and then click on the OK button.

This takes you to cell F4, the top left part of the block.

Next you should amend the details in this block.

● Type in a new label Sale for cell F4 and change the label in J6 from Cost to Amount.

● Centre the label in cell J6 using the alignment option in the Block notebook object inspector.

● In cell F8 type @DATE(91,12,28) for the date 28 December 1991.

The correct date format should now appear because the block you copied from had this cell formatted for the date format.

● Click on cell G8 and type 90, the number of shares, and click on H7 and type 0.84, the price of shares.

The broker's commission in cell I8 has automatically been calculated for you. Observe the formula in this cell and see how the reference point to the commission rate which is stored in cell F3 is preserved because of its absolute status in the formula. It should read +G8*H8*$A:$F$3.

● Click on cell F3 and type in a new commission rate of 5%.

This will change the commissions in both the Purchase and Sale blocks.

● Work out a formula for cell J8 to calculate the amount received from the share sale. If you do not arrive at the figure £71.82 in the cell then read on.

● The formula is +G8*H8–I8, which is the price per share multiplied by the number sold, less the commission.

● Now type in the next two rows of data to replace the figures copied from cells A8 to B10:

In cell	type
F9	The @DATE (94,6,20)
G9	The number 300
H9	The number 1.45
F10	The @DATE (93,1,15)
G10	The number 100
H10	The number 1.4.

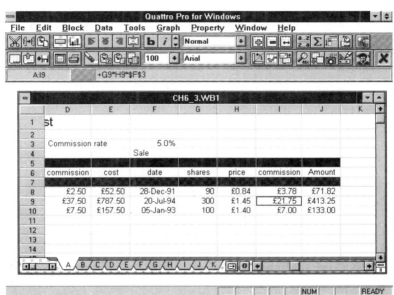

Screen dump 6.4

● Now copy the formulae from I8 and J8 to cells J9 and J10.

The active area of your spreadsheet, as shown in **Screen dump 6.4**, now goes further to the right than your screen allows you to see and you will have to move around your spreadsheet to see your work. The block named 'Sales' will be moved below the block named 'Purchase' later on.

However much planning is done there is often a need to re-design a spreadsheet. There are many ways of shunting things around. For now you will concentrate on the move command to bring the sales block down below the purchase block allowing the data on the spreadsheet to be better observed. **Screen dump 6.5** shows the effect this will have, leaving all data visible without you needing to move out of any area of the spreadsheet or creating a window.

— 6.5 Dragging a block around the — spreadsheet

One obvious method to do this is to use the Move and Copy options from the Block pull-down menu. The Move option places the highlighted block into the Clipboard and removes the cells from the spreadsheet at the same time. You would then move the cell pointer to where you want it moved and use the Paste option from the Edit pull-down menu. The technique is almost identical to Copy and Paste. Quattro Pro also allows you to move a block around like a graphics object.

● Highlight the block that contains the sale information; i.e. cells F4 to J10.

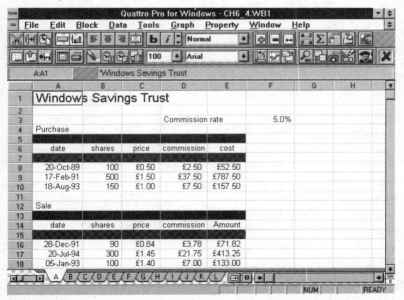

Screen dump 6.5

- Place the mouse pointer over the highlighted block and hold the left mouse button down without letting go. A small hand should now appear.

- Slowly move the mouse, without letting go of the button, and watch the entire block move with it.

- Move the block so that it is directly below the purchase block and starts at A12.

- Press the **Home** key on your keyboard to get a better view of the spreadsheet.

- If you cannot see the whole of your spreadsheet, click on the maximise button – the up arrow key on the top right of the notebook area.

The view you get should be similar to that shown in Screen dump 6.5.

6.6 The @IF function

You will now set up a section of the spreadsheet which will calculate the profit or loss of each share dealing and determine whether a gain is long-term or short-term. To be sure that you appreciate the nature of this problem, an explanation of the assumptions will first be stated.

The calculation of profit or loss is based on the difference of the final purchase price for each set of shares against the final selling price. It needs to be borne in mind that not all shares are sold off; hence it is not simply a formula of amount less cost.

The criterion for short-term or long-term gains will be whether the difference in the dates exceeds one year (365 days). If the dates are more than a year apart, then the gain or loss is long-term, otherwise it is short-term.

- type in the following labels:

F14	Gain (Loss)
G14	Term

- Extend the shaded block on 13 and 15 to columns F and G using the Copy and Paste commands.

Cell F16 is going to contain the degree of gain or loss. You will need to think carefully how this is worked out. You will need to get Quattro Pro to calculate how much you would have paid for the shares sold before you can determine the gain or loss. This will be the purchase price for the shares plus the commission, i.e. price shares sold for, less price paid for shares. Price shares sold for is the share selling price per share (cell C16) multiplied by the number sold (cell B16) less the commission. Price paid for shares is share purchase price per share (cell C8) multiplied by number sold (cell B16) plus the commission.

Think carefully about this before accepting the formula.

The formula is, therefore:

$$+B16*C16*(100\%-\$F\$3)-C8*B16*(100\%+\$F\$3)$$

● Type this formula into cell F16.

● Format the cell to currency to two decimal places.

● Click on cell A8 and alter the date to @DATE(91,7,30) to alter what appears in cell F16.

● Copy the formula and format in cell F16 to the block F17 to F18.

Now for the IF command that will determine whether the transaction is long-term or short-term. The logic of it goes something like this:

If the cell contents of the selling date is more than 365 greater than the purchase date then type in 'Long' into cell G16, else type in 'Short'.

● To achieve this, click on cell G16 and type:

@IF(A16-A8>365,"Long","Short").

The **If Statement** appears in brackets and is broken into three components.

The first part is the argument. In this case it was A16-A8>365, which calculates the value of cell A16 less the value of cell A8 (which are dates in number form) and determines if it greater than 365.

The second part appears after the first comma and is an instruction as to what should be done if the argument is true. In this instance it is to place the word 'Long' in the cell. The word **must** be typed between double inverted commas.

The third part appears after the second comma and is an instruction as to what should be done if the argument is false. In this instance it is to place the word 'Short' in the cell. Again, the word **must** be typed between the commas.

● Copy the formula in cell G16 to cells G17 to G18.

● Examine **Screen dump 6.6** to give you an idea of what you should now have achieved.

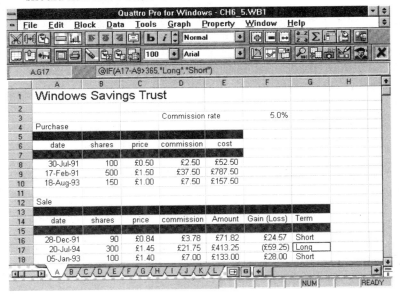

Screen dump 6.6

The last two entries made into your spreadsheet are complex and you may need time to ponder over them. Experiment for a while by:

Altering the commission rate

Altering the dates

Altering the purchase and selling prices of the shares.

● Save your spreadsheet as HST2 before moving on to the next section.

● Print out the spreadsheet, remembering to define the block to be printed and to preview your work before printing.

Finally, you will use another method for clearing your spreadsheet in preparation for the second part of this chapter. There are a number of ways of clearing the spreadsheet.

1 Highlight the entire spreadsheet and, from the Edit pull-down menu, click on Clear.

2 Highlight the entire spreadsheet and, from the Edit pull-down menu, click on Cut. This will also place the block contents into the Clipboard.

3 From the File pull-down menu click on Close.

4 Highlight any cells in each of the rows and, from the Block pull-down menu click on Delete and then choose Rows.

5 Highlight any cells in each of the columns and, from the Block pull-down menu click on Delete and then click on Columns.

● Highlight the entire spreadsheet and then press the **Delete** or **Del** key on your keyboard.

– 6.7 Relative and absolute formulae –

The next example uses a list of dates and numbers of caravans sold by a particular dealer over a particular year. See **Screen dump 6.7**. This example will give you further practice developing formulae and good presentation.

Each month a number of caravans are sold, such as 10 in August. They cost £2,000 each which is a total cost of £20,000. The 15% mark up gives a selling price of £2,300 per caravan. The profit is worked out as the difference between selling price and cost price multiplied by the number sold.

● Type the title **Caravan Sales for the Year** in cell A1 and then change (to your own taste) the font and point size of the title using the notebook object inspector.

● Highlight cells A1 to D1, and in the Block notebook object inspector click on the Line Drawing option.

● Select Outline, then the double line.

● Now click on OK to return to the spreadsheet.

● The column headings with cell locations are:

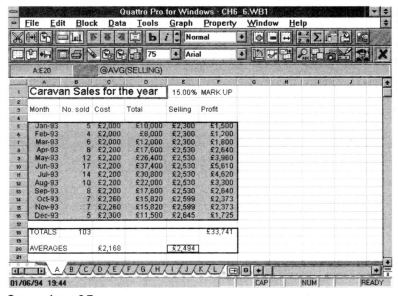

Screen dump 6.7

In cell	type
A3	Month
B3	No. Sold
C3	Cost
D3	Total
E3	Selling
F3	Profit

● Type in all the numbers sold in column B for the block of cells B5 to B16.

● Highlight cells B5 to B16.

● Click on Block, then on Names, then on Create. Give the highlighted block the name SOLD.

● In cell F1 type in the label Mark Up.

● In cell E1 type 15%. Now format this cell using Numeric Format from the Block notebook object inspector, set the format to Percent, to two decimal places, and click on OK.

Next you will type in a date in cell A5 and get the program to calculate the remaining months. In order to appreciate the usefulness of this facility it is wise to format the cells where the dates are to be typed before putting dates into them.

● Highlight cells A5 to A16.

● Activate the Block notebook object inspector, click on the Numeric Format option, then on the Date option.

● Click on the third option, date format MMM-YY, which will show only the month and year.

● In cell A5 type in the date for 1 January 1993 as @DATE(93,1,1).

● Now click on cell A6 and type in the formula +A5+31.

The purpose of this is to add 31 days to 1 January to go into February.

● Now copy the formula in cell A6 to the block A7 to A16.

Each consecutive month should appear from January to December. The principle is that each cell is 31 days greater than the cell above.

● At this stage, browse through the cells, examine each formula in the block A5 to A16 and be clear in your own mind how it works.

The concept of such formula copying always taking a relative set of values is an important one. Look again to see how the concept works.

● Type the cost figures into column C, using **Screen dump 6.7** as a guide.

● Click on cell D5 and type in a formula that will calculate the total cost of the caravans to the trader: +C5*B5.

● Now use Copy and Paste to copy the formula in cell D5 to the block D6 to D16.

Again, observe what has happened in the cells in this block. Each formula is a multiple of the cell two positions to the left and one to the left.

Now you will see where this principle is *not* what is wanted in determining the Selling Price. The formula you want in cell E5 is one that multiplies the Cost in cell C5 by the percentage mark-up set up in cell E1 added to the original cost:

(C5*E1)+C5

Note that the use of brackets ensures the multiplication is done first.

● Click on cell E5 and type in this formula.

● Now use the copy and paste commands to copy the formula in cell E5 to the block E6 to E16.

Something is wrong!

Observe the formula in this block of cells and you will see that the percentage to work with is always assumed to be four cells directly above. In fact, although this relative position has worked in your favour up until now, you want to fix the cell E1 in the formula. Define an absolute cell value by placing a $ (dollar) sign in front of the cell location; in other words instead of placing E1 in the formula place $E$1.

● Click on cell E5 and amend the formula to (C5*$E$1)+C5.

● Now use the copy and paste commands to copy the formula in cell E5 to the block E6 to E16.

You should now have the desired result.

On a technical note, only the second part (the row number) needed to be fixed as the column E bit would have stayed correct. Quattro Pro allows you to mix the absolute with relative references in a formula. In other words E$1 would have worked as well, making the formula (C5*E$1)+C5.

● To complete the spreadsheet, type in the formula (E5*B5)–D5 in cell F5 and copy this formula to the block F6 to F16.

● Highlight the block F5 to F16.

● From the Block menu click on Names and then click on Create. Give the highlighted block the name PROFIT.

● Click on cell A18 and type in the label TOTALS.

● Click on cell C18 and type in the function @SUM(COST).

● Click on cell F18 and type in the function @SUM(PROFIT).

● Click on cell A20 and type in label AVERAGES.

● Highlight the block C5 to C16.

- From the Block menu click on Names and then click on Create. Give the highlighted block the name COST.

- Click on cell C20 and type in the function @AVG(COST).

- Highlight the block E5 to E16 and name the block as SELLING.

- Click on cell E20 and type in the function @AVG(SELLING).

In order to tidy up your spreadsheet, do the following:

- Format all money figures to currency with zero decimal places and prefixed with a £.

- Highlight the block A5 to F16 and activate the Block notebook object inspector.

- Click on the Line Drawing option, and create a thick outline to the stock details data.

- Repeat this for the block A18 to F20.

- Now highlight the block A18 to F20 again and add shading.

- Finally, highlighting some of the block, use the Text Color and Shading options to add a little colour to your final spreadsheet.

- 6.8 Altering the spreadsheet screen -

This final part of the chapter will give you the opportunity to investigate some of the features of Quattro Pro and how you can remove much of the screen information. In doing so, you will use two object inspectors you have come across before.

First, you will alter some of the display options.

- Activate the spreadsheet properties object inspector by placing your mouse pointer on the title bar and clicking your right mouse button.

- Remove the ticks in the Display Options panel: Show Speeedbar; Show Input Line; and Show Status Line.

- Click on OK and examine the outcome.

Next, you will change some of the page properties.

- Now activate the Active Page object inspector by placing the mouse pointer of the page letter A at the bottom of your notebook and clicking the right mouse button again.

- Click on the Borders option and remove the Row Borders and Column Borders.

- Now click on Grid Lines and remove the Horizontal and Vertical lines.

- Now click OK and examine the results.

Screen dump 6.8 shows the effect of removing many of the attributes that make up the spreadsheet on your screen.

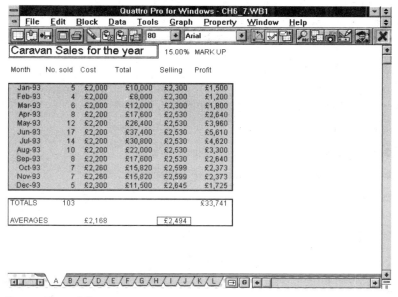

Screen dump 6.8

- Use Page Preview from the File pull-down menu to see what a print-out would look like.

- Highlight column A. From the Block pull-down menu click on the Insert option and insert a Column at column A so that the spreadsheet is moved away from the left edge

You will notice that if you do not have a colour printer, the page preview will display the output in black and white.

● Print the spreadsheet.

Playing around with the appearance like this has the added benefit of helping you get to grips with much of the-terminology used by Quattro Pro. As a useful practice, have a go at restoring the original features, but one at a time rather than in chunks.

● Save your spreadsheet for possible future reference and practice.

—————— **6.9 Chapter summary** ——————

As a brief concluding challenge to this chapter, try this problem:

Allow cell F18 (Total Profit) to be entered by the user. From this, the spreadsheet should determine the percentage mark-up that is needed to get this profit and will then state the price that should be charged for the caravans each month.

In this chapter you have:

● Manipulated text around the spreadsheet.

● Formatted blocks with dates and currencies.

● Entered dates and further manipulated them using the @DATE function.

● Copied relative and absolute formulae.

● Used the @IF function to make decisions.

● Moved blocks around.

● Had more practice using named blocks to build formulae.

● Altered the general appearance of the spreadsheet by removing display options.

7

-USING THE DATABASE-

———— 7.1 Aims of this chapter ————

This chapter examines the way Quattro Pro allows you to set up tables of data and then rearrange them into a different logical order. In doing so, it also examines a method whereby a table can be rearranged by a single operation from the keyboard rather than performing a whole string of command entries through the Quattro Pro menus and object inspectors.

In many ways it is useful to extract specific information from a data table, such as a list of all unsold houses in a list of house details held by an estate agent. This example is developed in the latter part of this chapter.

—— 7.2 Setting out a database table ——

Screen dump 7.1 will show you what you are trying to achieve in this chapter.

With one key stroke an entire table can be rearranged to sort a list by, for example, Name, Date of Birth, or Salary.

Before starting it is worth making yourself familiar with some of the jargon that this chapter will introduce you to.

A database can be defined as a collection of pieces of information organised in a meaningful way. Consider a phone directory, which lists names, addresses, and phone numbers. In the phone book, these data are arranged in a table of three columns. Each entry in the phone book is thus divided into three parts: name, address, phone number. In technical terms, each entry in the phone book is called a 'record'; each section into which each record is divided is called a 'field'. Once you have grasped these concepts, you are well on your way to understanding what databases are about.

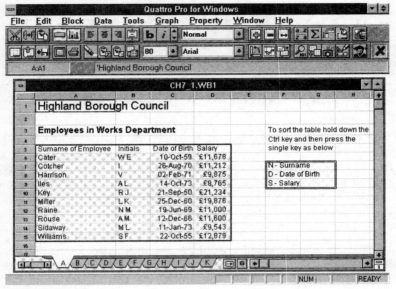

Screen dump 7.1

——— 7.3 Typing in record details ———

● Create a new spreadsheet and start by making sure the following settings are in place:

Page Properties

    Columns and Row Borders

Spreadsheet Properties

    Input Line

    Speedbar

    Status Line

These may be missing if you did not change them back after the work you did in the last chapter.

● Now type in the required header labels.

Cell	Label
A1	Highland Borough Council
A3	Employees in Works Department
A5	Surname of Employee
B5	Initials
C5	Date of Birth
D5	Salary

● Widen columns A and C.

● Enhance the heading and sub-headings to suit your taste.

Next you will need to type in the details of each individual employee. Each row (or line) on the spreadsheet represents a record of an employee with the cell locations holding fields: Surname, Initials, Date of Birth and Salary.

● Type in the record details from **Screen dump 7.1**, remembering that dates will have to be typed in using the function @DATE(year, month, day). Then you will have to format the date using the Format option from the Block notebook object inspector.

● Type in the salary figures and, using the Numeric Format option from the Block notebook object inspector, format the figures to Currency and to zero decimal places.

At this point it may be worth your while typing in the records in a different and unsorted order to those listed in **Screen dump 7.1**, which are in Surname order.

● Now type in cell F3.

To sort the table hold down the Ctrl key and the press the single key as below:

The text will go off the edge of the screen, so:

● Highlight the block F3 to H5.

● Click on Block from the menu bar, then on Reformat.

● Click OK.

● Type in the following:

In cell	type
F7	N – Surname
F8	D – Date of Birth
F9	S – Salary

● Using the Block notebook object inspector, highlight the block F7 to G8 and shade the block in light yellow.

● Create a thick line around the outer edge of the database area, from A5 to D15, to distinguish it clearly from the rest of the noteboook area.

To recap on the database features, you have:

1 The column heading representing the field name.

2 Each field name unique.

3 Each record kept on one row.

● Shade the database block A6 to D15 in light blue.

—————— 7.4 Sorting the records ——————

Before beginning with the sort, you should NAME certain parts of your spreadsheet in order to conform to better spreadsheet practice and to get a better 'feel' for the concept of a database.

● Alter the surname in the first record from Cater to Smith. This will help you see the effect of the sorting better.

● Highlight cells A6 to D15.

● Click on Block from the menu bar and then click on Name followed by clicking on Create.

● Now type in the block name as DATABASE and click on OK.

● You should now repeat this for the blocks in each column:

Block	Name
A6..A15	SURNAME
B6..B15	INITIALS

C6..C15	DATE OF BIRTH
D6..D15	SALARY

The next task is to rearrange the records into surname order.

● Click on Data from the menu-bar.

From the options available, you want to sort the records into order.

● Click on Sort to reveal an object inspector.

At this point you need to define where on the spreadsheet the database block is and how you want it sorted. Observe **Screen dump 7.2** to see how the settings have been made.

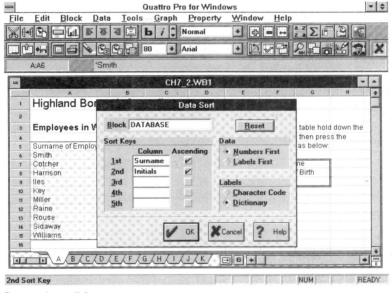

Screen dump 7.2

Having defined where the database block is, the next stage is to indicate by what field you want to sort the records by, i.e. the 1st Sort key.

● Ensure the data Block is typed in as DATABASE.

● Type in SURNAME as the block that contains the 1st Sort key.

You will also have to decide in what order you want the records; i.e. ascending or descending.

- Leave the tick adjoining the block name to indicate you want the data sorted in Ascending order. If no such tick exists, place one in the box by clicking on it.

In the event that two surnames are the same, you want to decide on what basis to sort the common records by. This is when you need to define a 2nd Sort key.

Instead of using your mouse, you can get to the section by pressing the Alt and 2 keys simultaneously. If you observe the object inspector that appears in **Screen dump 7.2** you will see that many of the characters are underlined. Holding down the **Alt** key and pressing one of these keys to get there has the same effect as highlighting the option with your mouse and clicking.

- Type in INITIALS as the block that contains the 2nd Sort key and again leave the tick adjoining the block name to indicate you want the data sorted in Ascending order. If no such tick exists, place one in the box by clicking on it.

- Now click on OK to see the effect.

In **Screen dump 7.2** there were two other panels in the object inspector which can also be altered to affect the way the sorting is carried out.

The Data panel determines whether Numbers or Labels should take precedence. For example, if Numbers have precedence, then 100L will come before A110 while if Labels take precedence then this is reversed.

The Labels panel mainly affects the role of capital letters. If the setting is by Character Code, then lower case letters will come before upper case. In other words, zebra comes before Aardvark. If the setting is Dictionary then the case of the label will be ignored. In the example you are working with, it is the Dictionary setting that you want.

Experiment with this by changing some of the surnames so that they are no longer in alphabetical order and repeat the process.

Before moving on, it is worth seeing the effect of inserting more data into the database.

- Highlight the cells A14 to A15.

- Click on Block from the menu bar, click on Insert and then click on Rows.

● Press the Enter key(as opposed to using your mouse to accept OK).

● Now type in the following two records:

Surname	initials	Date of Birth (using @DATE)	Salary
Adams	C D	12 July 1972	9450
Winterton	D P	10 November 1969	10420.

● Now sort the database again, clicking on <u>D</u>ata from the menu bar, clicking on <u>S</u>ort followed by simply pressing the **Enter** key.

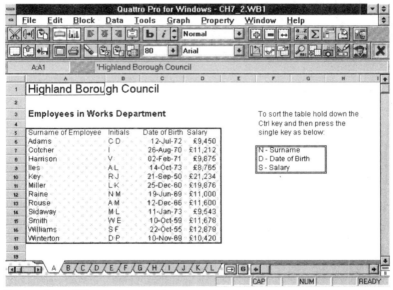

Screen dump 7.3

—— 7.5 Creating and using macros ——

The next stage is to build a facility into the spreadsheet whereby an operator does not have to type in such a sophisticated sequence of commands in order to alter the logical sequence of records on the screen as and when needed. In other words, you want to replace a sequence of commands with just one key stroke.

What you will need to get to grips with is the idea of creating a macro: a facility of storing a whole set of commands somewhere on a spreadsheet that can be activated by an operator with only one command.

The stages are

1. Store the macro somewhere on the spreadsheet, preferably out of sight.

2. Get the program to record the steps made to sort the database.

3. Name the macro.

4. Create the icon that will be used to activate the macro identifying the name of the macro.

You can now create the first of these macros to sort the database records by Name order in the stages indicated.

● Click on Tools from the menu bar and then click on the Macro option.

● Now click on Record to start recording your steps.

● Type in cell reference A90 as the Location to store the macro and click on OK.

At this stage you have instructed Quattro Pro to record all the next steps and store these details starting at cell A90. The next stage is actually to carry out the sorting of the database.

● Click on the Data option from the menu bar and click on Sort.

● Type in DATABASE as the data block, irrespective of whether it has already been typed in.

● Type in SURNAME as the 1st sort key and INITIALS as the 2nd sort key, again irrespective of whether they have already been typed in.

● Now click on OK to activate the sort.

● Click on Tools from the menu bar and then click on Macro.

● Now click on Stop Record to stop the recording.

The final stage is to name the macro so that it can be used.

● Press function key **F5** and type in the cell reference A90 as the place where the macro has been stored.

● Click on OK and you will go to the recorded macro.

● Now highlight cells A90..A95 where the macro has been stored.

● Click on <u>B</u>lock from the menu bar, then on <u>N</u>ames, followed by <u>C</u>reate. Type in the block name as \N noting that you have to use the \ (backslash) key.

● Click on OK.

● Press the **Home** key to return to cell A1.

You are now ready to activate this macro.

● Activate the macro by holding down the **Ctrl** key and pressing the N key once.

Next you need a macro to sort the database into Date of Birth order.

● Click on <u>T</u>ools from the menu bar, then on <u>M</u>acro, then on <u>R</u>ecord.

● Type in cell reference C90 as the Location to store the macro and click on OK.

● Click on the <u>D</u>ata option from the menu bar and click on <u>S</u>ort.

● Type in DATABASE as the data block again, irrespective of the fact that it has already been typed in.

● Type in DATE OF BIRTH as the 1st sort key and SURNAME as the 2nd sort key.

● Now click on OK to activate the sort.

● Click on <u>T</u>ools, then on <u>M</u>acro, then click on Stop <u>R</u>ecord to stop the recording.

● Use function key F5 to go to cell C90.

● Now highlight cells C90..C93 where the macro has been stored and then name the block as \D.

And finally you want a macro to sort names by Salary order.

● Click on <u>T</u>ools from the menu bar, then on <u>M</u>acro, then on <u>R</u>ecord.

● Type in cell reference F90 as the location to store the macro and click on OK.

● Click on the <u>D</u>ata option from the menu bar and click on <u>S</u>ort.

- Type in DATABASE as the data block again, irrespective of the fact that it has already been entered.

- Type in SALARY as the 1st sort key and SURNAME as the 2nd sort key and click on OK.

- Click on Tools from the menu bar and then click on Macro.

- Now click on Stop Record to stop the recording.

- Use function key F5 to go cell F90.

- Name the block F90 to F93 as \S.

- Press the **Home** key on your keyboard to return to cell A1.

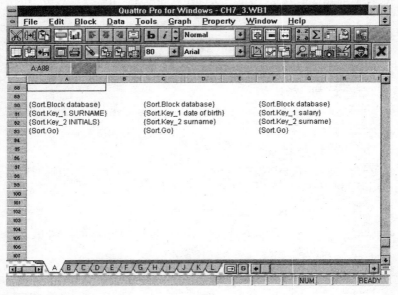

Screen dump 7.4

Screen dump 7.4 shows what you should have at this stage with the three macros that have been set up in this exercise.

- Experiment with the three macros before moving on to the next section.

- 7.6 Creating your own macro button -

You will only be able to take advantage of this section if you are using version 4 or higher. If you are unable to do this, then skip to section 7.7.

On the speedbar is a series of buttons that allows you to perform a whole series of operations quickly and in many cases will bypass the need to use menus and object inspectors. In this section of the chapter, you will have the opportunity to create your own such buttons that will perform similar short cuts.

If you observe Screen dump 7.5 you will see that the table to the right of the database has been replaced by three buttons that perform the sorts. Simply point your mouse pointer over the required button and click the left button.

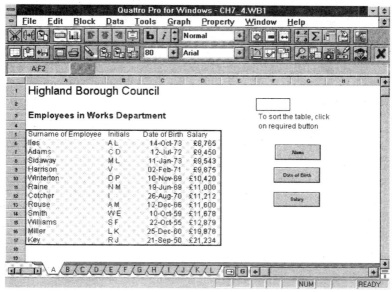

Screen dump 7.5

● Amend the text in the cells F3 to F5 to read:

  To sort the table click on required button.

● Now highlight cells F7 to G9, click on <u>E</u>dit from the menu bar, then on Cl<u>e</u>ar.

The option Clear will clear all contents and any formats, font changes and lines associated with the block while Clear Contents will only clear the data in the cells.

You are now ready to enter the macro buttons.

● Place the mouse pointer over the macro button icon on the top speedbar, the fourth icon from the left.

● A small icon with ABC in it will appear that is controlled by your mouse. Move this to the right of the database table and click your left mouse button.

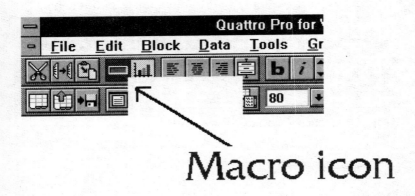

Macro icon

At this stage, a button will appear on the spreadsheet. This button will 'float' on the spreadsheet in that if it appears on top of occupied cells, they will not have their contents affected. This button can be moved and have its size altered in the same way as any other object. The next stage, however, will be to type in a label on the button and assign it the sort macro.

● Place your mouse pointer over the button and click the right button on your mouse.

Now a menu will appear that is related to the button. You want to alter the button properties.

● Click on Button Properties and then click on Label Text.

- Type in the label Name in the resulting object inspector and click on OK.

- Now recall this button object inspector with your right mouse button and, from the button properties, click on Macro.

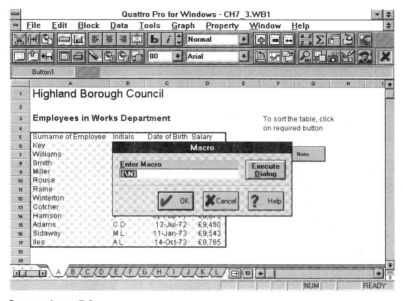

Screen dump 7.6

You now need to type in the macro that will be assigned to this button. In **Screen dump 7.6** you will see how the setting is made. It is important that when doing so the macro to be defined is placed between curly brackets { }.

- Type in the macro definition \N as shown in **Screen dump 7.6.**

- Now experiment by clicking on the button.

- With the macro icon from the speedbar, create two more macro buttons and set them up to activate the two new macros of DATE OF BIRTH and SALARY with their respective object inspectors.

- Alter the Label Text on each macro button to that shown in **Screen dump 7.5.**

- Now save your work with the name 'dbase1'.

By now you should have gained a reasonable understanding of what a macro is and how to set one up and use it. The next section of this chapter will give some more details about the database facilities contained within Quattro Pro.

– 7.7 Using data query on a database –

In this part of the chapter you will use the Data Query part of the program to extract certain specified items from a list. Examine **Screen dump 7.7**.

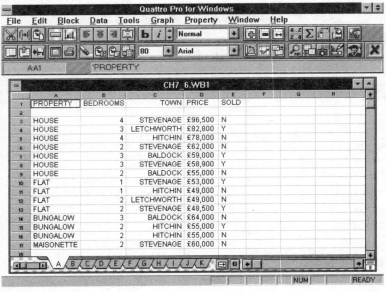

Screen dump 7.7

The aim is quite simple: to extract from the table a list of all those houses that have not been sold. Start by acquainting yourself with some more jargon. What you do is set up an output block table to which you will copy all the required data. The Criterion Section will represent the table that tells Quattro Pro the basis of the decision about which data to extract from the Database Block.

● Begin by typing all the details into a new spreadsheet. You will need to widen some columns.

In **Screen dump 7.7** the Alignment option from the notebook objector inspector was used to align the town names in column C to the right of their cells. Also the prices are displayed in £s.

At this stage the Database Block is the area from cell A1 to cell E17. Each row (house details) represents a single record in the database, while each cell in a row represents a field. You have 15 records from row 3 to row 17 and each record has five fields from column A to column E. This is a simple principle well worth getting used to. At the top of each column is the field name, which will have an important part to play in the demonstration.

● Click on Data from the menu bar, then on Query.

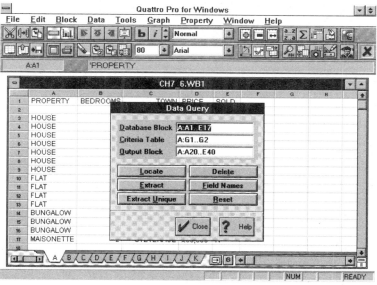

Screen dump 7.8

Screen dump 7.8 shows the resulting dialogue box with the various settings for the Database Block, Criteria Table, and Output Block. Before you can actually move forward on this, you will need to set some more data on the spreadsheet to perform Query commands.

The Database Block is the database itself where the computer is going to look for the records. Here it is A1..E17. It is important to note that the Database Block must include the field names at the top of the column. This is different from the database used earlier in this chapter to sort data, which excluded the field names.

———— 7.8 Defining criteria and ———— output blocks

● Return to your spreadsheet.

The next stage is to type in details about a Criterion Block. This is what the program needs to determine what you want extracted from the database block. In the present example you want to extract details of all unsold houses.

● Set up the Criterion Block by first typing in the following:

In cell	type
G1	SOLD
G2	N

This establishes the criterion as those records where the field name SOLD has an N entered.

You also need to set the Criterion Block, in other words, where the criterion appears on the spreadsheet.

It is important that the Criterion Block includes the field name that appears at the top of the column where the data are held.

The next stage is to decide where to put records you extract. This is called the Output Block.

● Type in the following details in their respective cells:

In cell	Location Label
A20	PROPERTY
B20	BEDROOMS
C20	TOWN
D20	PRICE
E20	SOLD.

When defining the Output Block it is important to give ample rows below the field headings so that there is room for the house records that match the criterion defined. You can place the Output Block anywhere on the spreadsheet, including a different page. By placing it underneath the database query block, it has the advantage of the column-widths being set up correctly to suit the data, although there is no imperative need for this.

You will also observe that the Output Block needs the field names at the top. Each field name must match one in the database query block. The field names do not have to be in the same order; neither does every field defined.

—— 7.9 Extracting the required data ——

● Click on <u>D</u>ata from the menu bar, then on Query, and then type in the block details as in **Screen dump 7.8**, namely:

Database Block	'	A1..E17
Criterion Table		G1..G2
Output Block		A20..E40.

● Click on <u>E</u>xtract.

● Now return to the spreadsheet by clicking on Close.

As a result of this action you should have the results as shown in **Screen dump 7.9**.

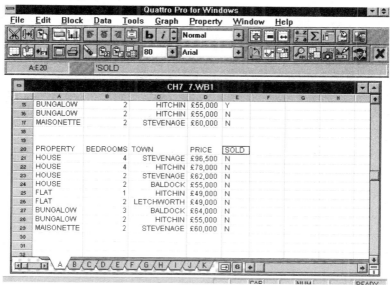

Screen dump 7.9

Now try the following:

● Redefine your Criterion Block as:

Cell	Label
G1	PRICE
G2	(D3<64000)

● Click on <u>D</u>ata from the menu bar, then on <u>Q</u>uery.

● Click on <u>E</u>xtract again (the earlier block settings will not have been altered) and click on Close to return to the spreadsheet.

This has the effect of extracting all houses with a price of less than £64,000. Having typed this formula into the cell you will see that the number 1 appears in the cell. This indicates that the condition is false; in other words, that the cell value is NOT less than 64000. When you extract from this, the operation knows that it needs to perform this throughout the database query block.

Now try the following:

● Redefine your Criterion Block as:

In cell	type
G1	PRICE
G2	(D3>64000#AND#D3<75000)

● Click on Data from the menu bar, then on Query.

● Click on Extract again (the earlier block settings will not have been altered) and click on Close to return to the spreadsheet.

This will extract those houses whose price is greater than £60,000 and less than £75,000 – a common type of request from a database needed in such circumstances.

Next, you will see how two criteria can be set up.

● Type in your Criterion Block as

In cell	type
G1	PROPERTY
G2	HOUSE
H1	BEDROOMS
H2	(B3>2)

- Click on Data from the menu bar, then on Query. Type in the Criteria Table as G1..H2.

- From this object inspector click on the Extract option followed by clicking on Close.

The effect should be to extract those properties which are houses with more than two bedrooms and place them all in the Output Block.

— 7.10 Deleting specified records —

Before going any further, it would be wise to save your spreadsheet in case you ever want to refer to it. Before deleting records, it is often a good idea to save the current version of the spreadsheet in case it is needed again.

- Type in the following label details in your spreadsheet to redefine the Criteria section:

In cell	type
G1	SOLD
G2	Y

- Click on Data from the menu bar, then on Query.

- Click on Extract again This will place into the Output Table a copy of those fields whose houses have been sold.

- Now go back to the spreadsheet and type N in cell G2.

- Click on Data from the menu bar, then on Query.

- Now click on Delete, then on Close.

- As a precaution, you will be asked whether you want to cancel the request or go ahead and delete it. Click on Delete.

This will have the effect of deleting from the Database Block all records that match the Criteria Table. In other words, it will remove all records that have N in the SOLD field.

When you delete there is no going back other than reverting to a spreadsheet file you have already saved. You will see that all the records with N in the SOLD field appear in the output table while all records with Y in the SOLD field appear in the input table.

—— 7.11 Data query locate, extract —— unique and field names

The Data Query object inspector allows four options: Locate, Extract, Extract Unique, and Field Names. Up until now, you have Extracted data from the Database Block, placed results to the Output Block or deleted records from the Database Block.

Locate allows you to search through the Database Block to find a record that matches the conditions of the Criteria Table.

Extract Unique does exactly the same as Extract except it does not repeat records that are the same.

Field Names assigns block names to fields so that you can use them in search formulas.

Reset will reset the Database Block, Criteria Table, and Output Block in the Data Query object inspector.

Many of the other data facilities that appear within the data pull-down menu refer to links and activities on data tables and databases external to the spreadsheet you are working in. It is beyond the scope of a book of this nature to cover these parts of the package and would be something developed at a more advanced level.

— 7.12 Further work with a database —

In this third example you will set up a simple stock database, from it, sort the records into value or stock reference order, and print a list using a macro.

To get yourself started, examine **Screen dump 7.10** to see what kind of layout is required and the cell entries you want, observing the following points before you type in values, formulae, and formats.

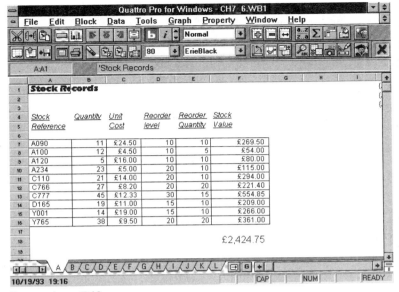

Screen dump 7.10

● The field Stock Reference contains labels.

● The fields Quantity, Unit Cost, Reorder Level, and Reorder Quantity are numeric entries.

● The Stock Value field is a formula: Quantity multiplied by Unit Cost. (Both need to be formatted for currency to two decimal places.)

● Cell F18 is a @SUM function summing all Stock Values.

● The following blocks are NAMED. Click on Block, Names, and Create.

Block	Name
A7..F16	Stock Data
A7..A16	Reference
B7..B16	Quantity
C7..C16	Unit Cost
D7..D16	Minimum Level
E7..E16	Reorder Quantity
F7..F16	Stock Value

- From the Block notebook object inspector both Line drawing and Font options have been used to improve the presentation of the database.

- The grid lines have been removed using the Page object inspector.

Such presentation will have no detrimental effect to the subsequent database activities.

—— 7.13 Recording commands ——

In this final section you will create a macro to sort the table by value.

- Click on Tools from the menu bar and then click on the Macro option.

- Now click on Record to start recording your steps.

Quattro Pro now needs to know where on the spreadsheet the macro is to be stored. Any place where the macro will not interfere with your work will do. As before, the macro is best stored out of sight.

- Type in cell reference A100 as the location and click on OK.

- Click on Data from the menu bar and then click on Sort.

- Type in STOCK DATA as the data Block and type in REFER-ENCE as the 1st Sort key.

- Now click on OK to activate the sort.

- Click on Tools from the menu bar and the click on Macro.

- Now click on Stop Record to stop the recording.

You have now created the macro. If the macro does not work exactly as required, then it can be edited like any other cell entry.

- Go to cell A100 using the function key **F5**.

The resulting macro should look something like that shown in **Screen dump 7.11**

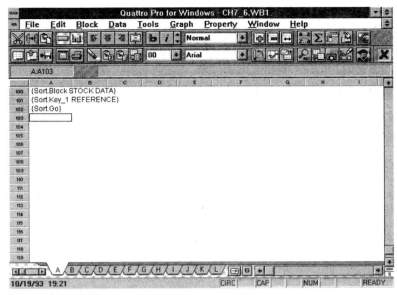

Screen dump 7.11

● Highlight the block where the macro is stored and, clicking on Block, Names, name the block as SORT.

● Now return to cell A1 using your Home key and, using the macro icon on the speedbar, create an icon button that will activate the macro.

——— 7.14 Chapter summary ———

As a final exercise, have a go at the following:

1 Produce a macro recording the commands to sort the table into reference number order.

2 Use Data Query to set up the following:

A Database Block consisting of all records and field names

A Criteria Table to extract all those stocks that have a quantity below minimum order level

An Output Block below the database

3 Write a macro that extracts all stock records from the database that are below the minimum stock level and places them in the Output Block.

4 Write a macro to print the Output Block only.

5 When you have done this and tried the macros, record the use of these macros and define a fourth macro that activates, in the above sequence, the use of the other three macros.

This chapter has covered many aspects of database activity although a good deal of it has been left out. The activities that have been left out are the more advanced features of the database utilities and beyond the scope of a book like this, which has been written as an introduction to the package.

In this chapter, you will have:

● Defined the term database.

● Typed in a structured database with records on rows and field titles at the tops of columns.

● Sorted records into a logical sequence.

● Set up, named and activated a macro.

● Set up a Query and extracted data from a defined Input Block into an Output Block using a given criterion.

● Located a record from an Input Block using a given criterion.

● Deleted records from an Input Block using a given criterion.

● Recorded a sequence of commands, stored them on to the spreadsheet and created a macro from it.

8

MORE ON GRAPHS AND CHARTS

──── 8.1 Aims of this chapter ────

This chapter aims to give you the opportunity further to develop your knowledge and skill with regard to graphs and charts beyond those built up in Chapters 4 and 5. Quattro Pro offers a wide range of facilities in graphs and charts, with varying types and varying presentation. There is also an annotation facility which allows you to indicate information more powerfully.

At this stage in the book it is assumed that the reader knows how to set up a spreadsheet and produce a graph. If you have forgotten any points, refer to the previous chapters.

The graphs created in this chapter will also be needed when you get to the next chapter, which will develop the graphics yet further.

──── 8.2 More on bar charts ────

This section examines bar charts using a different example from those previously used and allows you to show data in different perspectives.

Screen dump 8.1 shows a spreadsheet of an insurance company's premiums over a given year.

Remember, you cannot simply copy the figures in the spreadsheet. Note the following with regard to the data.

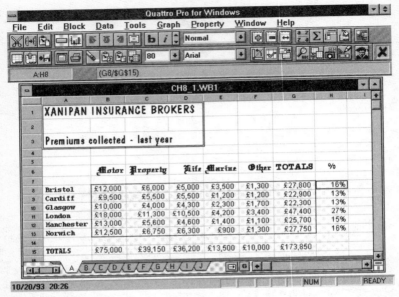

Screen dump 8.1

- Totals are established using the @SUM function.

- All monetary values are formatted in currency with zero places of decimals.

- Percentages are established using a formula. The formula in cell H8 is: +G8/$G$15 and in cell B17 is: +B15/$G$15. The dollar sign in the formula sets an absolute cell reference. This was discussed at length in Chapter 6.

- The values that appear in the cells are then formatted to per cent, to zero decimal places.

Once you have typed in the spreadsheet data, you can work on the graphs.

Graph 8.1 shows a graph that is no different in construction from the one set up in Chapter 4, except that it is not three dimensional. However, it will prove a useful starting-point. As a general principle, use the following procedure for preparing a graph.

First create a set of named Blocks as a means of improving the way you will create graphs. You will be able to create graph block names without constantly going back to the spreadsheet and highlighting cells.

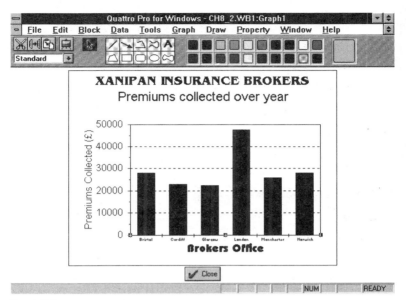

Graph 8.1

● Click on the <u>B</u>lock option from the menu bar, then on <u>N</u>ames, then on <u>C</u>reate.

● Type in the first Block Name in the object inspector LOCATION as the block A8..A13. Click on OK when done.

● Type in the remaining block details as follows:

Names	Block(s)
TYPES	B6..F6
TOTAL-TYPE	B15..F15
TOTAL-OFFICE	G8..G13
MOTOR	B8..B13
PROPERTY	C8..C13
LIFE	D8..D13
MARINE	E8..E13
OTHER	F8..F13

BRISTOL	B8..F8
CARDIFF	B9..F9
GLASGOW	B10..F10
LONDON	B11..F11
MANCHESTER	B12..F12
NORWICH	B13..F13

● Click on cell A20 and then click on the <u>B</u>lock option from the menu bar.

● Now click on <u>N</u>ames, then on <u>M</u>ake Table.

● In the Name Table Block, type A20, then click on OK.

You will get a list of these Block Names and references.

● Use the function key F5 to get to cell A20.

● Use **Screen dump 8.2** to check that you have correctly named the blocks and that the ranges they represent are correct. While doing this, set out the table with lines around them and shade them.

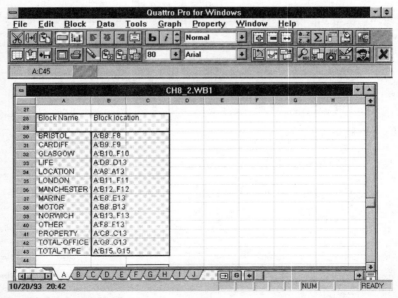

Screen dump 8.2

This method of naming blocks is designed to conform to good spreadsheet practice by making the setting up of the graphs easier to follow.

● Press the **Home** key on your keyboard to position the pointer at cell A1.

● Click on Graph from the menu bar and then click on New. The Graph Name will be Graph1.

A graph object inspector will now appear requiring you to define the X-Axis and at least a 1st Series range.

● Type in the following blocks details:

Series range

| X-Axis | LOCATION |
| 1st | TOTAL-OFFICE |

● Click on OK and inspect your graph.

At this stage you have a single Y variable which is defined as the 1st series with the data contained in the named range TOTAL-OFFICE. The next stage ought to be to type in various titles so that it becomes clear what the graph is representing.

● Click on Graph from the menu bar and then click on Titles and type in the following titles:

Main Title:	XANIPAN INSURANCE BROKERS
Subtitle:	Premiums collected over year
X-Axis Title:	Brokers Office
Y1-Axis Title:	Premiums Collected (£)

and then click on OK.

At this stage you will probably notice that labels and titles are not appearing in full on the screen. This is because their font sizes are too large. You need to reduce the font sizes of both the Main Title and X-Axis labels.

● Position the mouse pointer over the main title.

● Click your left mouse button once.

Small boxes should appear around the title to indicate that this has now become the object on which you wish to perform various activities.

- Now click your right mouse button to activate the relevant object inspector.

- Click on Font and reduce the *size* of the font. You also have the opportunity of altering the font itself from a list of available fonts.

- When you have done this, click on OK to see the result.

- Now repeat the exact process for the labels at the foot of each bar. They are probably too large for all of them to be visible; hence they need reducing in size.

──────── **8.3 Multiple bar charts** ────────

The problem with the graph as it stands is that it fails to show all the information that is available in the spreadsheet. The totals show which brokers are the largest but the graph does not break down the size of the business in each category as shown in the spreadsheet.

Look at **Graph 8.2** to see a graph which instead of showing the totals for each office shows the size of each category for each office.

There are in fact few differences between the two graphs beyond the stark appearances. The titles are still the same and the X-Axis has not been altered. One problem that has been taken away from you is the size of the scale. If you observe the Y-Axis you will see that the scale ranges from zero at the bottom to 18,000 at the top. In **Graph 8.1** the scale range was from zero to 50,000. Quattro Pro works all this out for you.

Each City broker is represented by five bars, one for each category of insurance. The bar for each insurance category is explained at the bottom of the screen by the Legends. This is an added extra you ought to put on your graph if an observer is to understand what is being shown.

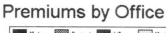

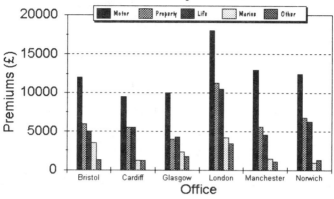

Graph 8.2

● Click on Graph from the menu bar then click on New and give it the name Graph2.

● Using **Screen dump 8.3**, complete the object inspector in order to get the required graph settings. When done, click on OK.

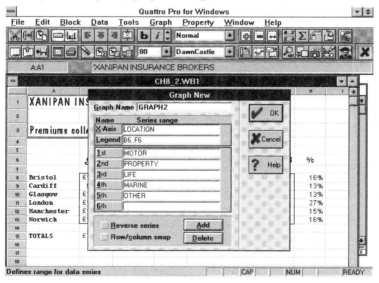

Screen dump 8.3

The settings set out in **Screen dump 8.3** now include a Legends range which is the range from B6 to F6. This is where the different types of insurance are labelled in the spreadsheet.

● Click on <u>G</u>raph from the menu bar and then type in the titles as follows:

<u>M</u>ain Title: Xanipan Insurance Brokers

Subtitle: Insurance Premiums by Office

<u>X</u> Axis Title: Office

Y<u>1</u> Axis Title: Premiums (£)

You will now need to reduce the fonts so that all text can be seen. You may also find that the Legend has obscured a part of your graph.

● Click the left button of your mouse over any text you want altered, including the Legends. Call up the object inspector and alter the size and style of font to ones you believe are best suited to the graph you have set up.

● If you wish to move the Legend bar, as has been done in Graph 8.2, then make the Legend the object with your mouse and, holding the left button of your mouse down, drag it up the screen.

On inspection, your graph should now show a desired result, although it is unlikely you are going to get an exact copy of the one that appears in **Graph 8.2**.

— 8.4 Changing the perspectives of — your graph

You now have a graph that shows, for each office, the premiums collected for each category of insurance. What if you want to show for each category of insurance how much each office collected? **Graph 8.3** shows an example of this.

Xanipan Insurance Brokers
Premiums by Type

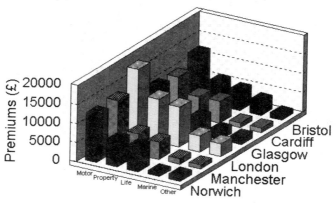

Graph 8.3

In this instance the X-Axis variable is the category of insurance while the Y-axis variables are the six city offices. You can now see the relative importance of each category of insurance more clearly and how much each office has contributed to the total.

To achieve this perspective of the data you need to alter the X and Y variables as well as the Legends. You will also have to change the Title on the X-axis. The rest will be much the same as before.

● Return to your spreadsheet via the Window menu and, clicking on Graph from the menu bar, create a new graph, Graph3.

● Observe **Screen dump 8.4** and type in the series as shown.

● Click on Graph from the menu bar and then click on Type.

● Now select the 3-D Bar graph.

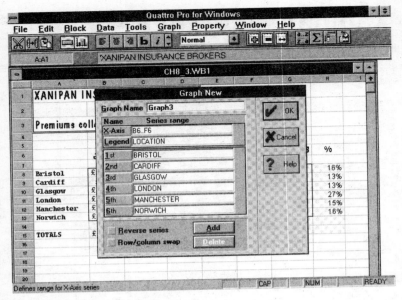

Screen dump 8.4

Your problem will be one of congestion. If you observe **Graph 8.3** you will see that the font sizes have been reduced for categories of insurance.

● Click on Graph and type in the following:

Main Title:	Xanipan Insurance Brokers
Subtitle:	Premiums by Type
Y1-Axis:	Premiums (£)

● Now use your mouse to activate object inspectors on the various parts of the graph to alter the fonts so that the congestion is avoided. Do not worry if you are unable to get an exact match with the one shown in **Graph 8.3**

Even when you get the desired 3-D effect you may find some of the bars a little obscured. In the next section you will see a possible alternative to this.

8.5 Stacked bar chart

Looking at **Graph 8.3** you may not be satisfied that the reader can tell at a glance the size of each category of insurance. Observe the stacked bar chart in **Graph 8.4** to see the data in a different way.

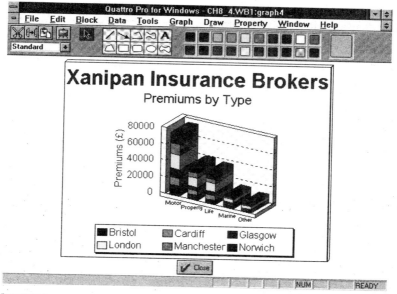

Graph 8.4

This graph uses one bar for each category on the X-Axis while splitting up the bar into components for each of the Y variables. Before generating this graph, you will use all the work you have done for Graph3 to help get to Graph4.

● Click on <u>G</u>raph, then on <u>C</u>opy.

● In the object inspector that appears, type in Graph3 in the From box and type Graph4 in the To box and then click on OK.

● Click on <u>G</u>raph, then on <u>E</u>dit. From here click on Graph4.

● Click on Graph, then on Type.

● Now click on 3-D Stacked Bar.

Everything has been done for you in terms of the scaling.

● Increase the size of the text that labels the insurance by type; it is all a little less congested.

Quattro Pro allows you to label particular parts of your graph. In this example, you will emphasise the premiums collected by the London office.

Quattro Pro also allows a very effective way of showing a graph where the bars are spilt into insurance types with a bar for each office.

● Copy Graph4 to Graph5 and then ensure you are editing Graph5.

● Click on Graph, then on Series.

● Now place a tick, using your mouse, in the Row/column swap box near the bottom of the object inspector.

● Click on OK and observe what you have been able to achieve quickly.

You will, of course, need to alter your subtitle to reflect what is being shown.

—— 8.6 The pie chart revisited ——

In order to get a different view of the data, you can produce a pie chart that shows first the share of total premium contribution by office and then the share of total premium by type. **Graph 8.5** shows both such graphs. These graphs were generated and named as Graph6 and Graph7 and then both inserted on to the spread-sheet.

You can see at a glance the relative contribution each has made to the total. In the Pie that shows Insurance by Broker, the London segment has been removed from the rest of the pie like a slice of cake being cut, a technique called 'exploding'. This can be extremely useful if you wanted to highlight one particular segment.

In order to create a pie chart, a little less information is required than was needed for the bar charts. All you need is an X variable that is used to determine what each portion of the pie represents and a variable to determine which figures to measure against. You also need titles at the top.

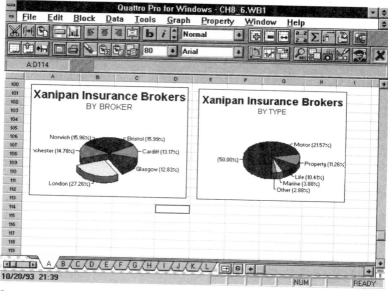

Graph 8.5

● Create a Graph6 and type in the following series:

Name	Series range
X	LOCATION
1st	TOTAL-OFFICE

● Now, with the graph object inspector, click on the 3-D Pie.

● Click on <u>G</u>raph, then on <u>T</u>itles.

● Type in following titles:

Main Title:	XANIPAN INSURANCE BROKERS
Subtitle:	BY BROKERS

If you observe **Graph 8.5** you will see that the London slice has been exploded from the rest.

● Position your mouse pointer over the segment that represents the London office and click your left mouse button once.

The small squares should appear around the segment, making this the object to work on.

● Now click your right mouse key button to reveal the Pie Graph Property object inspector for this part of the pie.

● Click on the Explode button and change the distance to 50% (100% will remove the segment completely from the pie).

● Click on OK and observe your work.

This is the first pie chart. Now create the next pie chart.

● Create a Graph7 and type in the following series:

Name	Series range
X	TYPES
1st	TOTAL-TYPE

● Type in the following titles:

Main title:	XANIPAN INSURANCE BROKERS
Subtitle:	BY TYPE

● Now alter the graph type to 3-D Pie as you did before.

● Now return to your spreadsheet by closing this graph screen.

Finally, to achieve what appears in **Graph 8.5**, you need to position yourself in the spreadsheet at a place away from where you are holding the all important data and Insert your graphs on to the spreadsheet.

● Return to the spreadsheet and position the cell pointer into cell A100 by pressing function key **F5** and typing in the cell reference.

● Click on Graph, then on Insert.

The small graphs icon that will appear is controlled with your mouse.

● Place the small icon over cell A100 and click the left button of your mouse.

● Now repeat this for Graph7, placing it at cell F100.

Now the graphs are on the sheet, they can be moved around to wherever you want them. You can move the graphs around with your mouse in exactly the same way as you move any block of cells.

——————— 8.7 Line graphs ———————

In this next section you will go on to develop a different set of
graphs for which the data you already have are not really appropriate. By means of extension, you will set up an additional table of
data showing the number of insurance claims made over the year
as well as the amount paid out to those claiming. Examine **Screen
dump 8.5** to see what you need to do to set up the initial data.

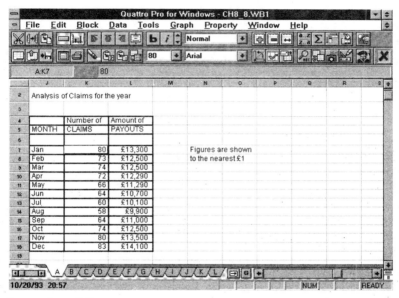

Screen dump 8.5

The table has been placed to the right of the other table and shows
two variables: Number of claims and Amount paid out, against one
time variable.

● Press function key **F5**, type J1 and press **Enter**.

● Type in the data exactly as it appears in **Screen dump 8.5**.
There are no formulae in this table.

● As has now become normal practice, name three of the blocks
by clicking on the <u>B</u>lock option, then on <u>N</u>ames, then on <u>C</u>reate.
The following Block Names need to be created:

Block(s)	Name
J7..J18	MONTH
K7..K18	CLAIMS
L7..L18	PAYOUTS

● Create a new graph as Graph8.

● Type in the following Series range:

X-Axis	MONTH
1st	CLAIMS

● Click on Graph from the menu bar, and then click on Type and, after clicking on the 2-D section, click on the Line graph.

● Click on Graph from the menu bar, then on Titles, and type in the following headings:

Main Title:	Xanipan Insurance Brokers
Subtitle:	Claim details for the year
X-Axis Title	MONTH
Y1-Axis Title	NUMBER OF CLAIMS

As with the bar charts, the scale has been worked out for you. You can see quite clearly how the of number claims made alters over the year.

● Use the relevant object inspectors to alter the font sizes of the X-Axis labels so that each of the months can be seen.

You are now in a position to type in the amount in £s claimed over the year and to place these details on to the same graph. Doing this will mean adding another variable. This will alter the scales quite considerably and will require labelling the Y-Axis to inform observers that it is used to measure both number of claims and amount in £s.

● Click on Graph from the menu bar and then click on Series and type in the 2nd Series name as PAYOUTS.

● Now take a look at the graph.

The problem should be an obvious one; you are unable to get a proper view of the number of claims because the Y-Axis covers too wide a range; from just 112 to over 15,000. You will need to reduce this range if you are to get a readable graph.

As a solution, you could express the amount claimed in thousands. This would reduce the range of numbers from 112 to 150. This will mean, however, creating a new range of values from which to plot on the spreadsheet. The method will involve creating a new column of figures and then hiding it from view.

- Go back to your spreadsheet, by closing the graph screen, and type into cell M7 the formula +L7/1000.

- Copy this formula to the block M8..M18.

- Click on Block from the menu bar and then click on Names and then click on Create. Type in the name PAYOUTS and alter the block to M7..M18.

- Now hide the newly created range. You can do this by clicking on Numeric Format in the notebook object inspector and clicking on Reveal/Hide. When defining what range to hide, type in the range name PAYOUTS rather than highlighting it.

- Click on Graph from the menu bar and then click on Edit. From here click on Graph8 from the list of graphs.

You should now see an improvement. The graph will need some alterations to improve its appearance.

- Click on Graph from the menu bar followed by Titles and amend the Y1-Axis label to read: Number of Claims/£000s.

- Click on Graph again and then click on Series and type in the Legend block as K5..L5:

To demonstrate further the flexibility of graph presentation, you will now change the graph type to a 3-D ribbon graph and alter its perspective.

- Click on Graph from the menu bar and then click on Type and on the Ribbon graph.

Graph 8.6 shows the three-dimensional effect with two ribbon lines representing the two variables. It serves as a useful demonstration of the power and flexibility Quattro Pro offers with respect to graphing.

- Place the mouse pointer inside the graph and click the left mouse button to make the graph itself the object

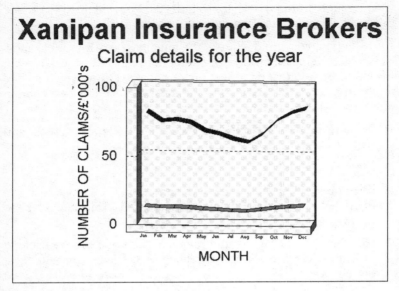

Graph 8.6

- Now click your right mouse button to activate the object inspector.

- Click on 3D View.

- Now rotate and elevate your graph by activating the arrow keys or slides that appear beneath the relevant text in the object inspector.

Screen dump 8.6 shows the settings that were made in order to arrive at the graph shown in **Graph 8.6**. You should spend some time practising with this as it is both fun and demonstrates how flexible the graphing can be.

Before going into the next section, it is worth examining a method by which you can determine the scale on the axis rather than having it automatically set. By example, you will set the Y-axis to go from zero up to 100: an extension at both the upper and lower ends of the axis.

- Click on Property from the menu bar and then click on the Y-Axis

- Now type in the Low scale value as 0 and type in the High scale value as 200.

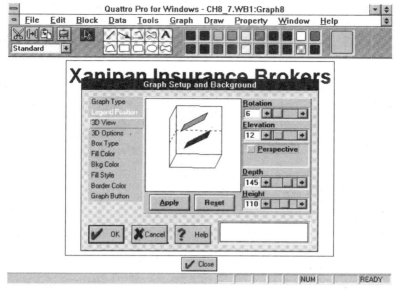

Screen dump 8.6

● Click on OK to see the effect.

Before moving on, look at the other line graphs that are available and spend time experimenting with their perspectives and the object inspectors that are available with each graph type.

—— 8.8 Scatter graphs or XY graphs ——

Such graphs are used to plot one variable against another in an attempt to see if there is any correlation. In other words, is there a relationship between one variable and another. For example, in the line graph you have just produced you plotted both number of claims and amount claimed against time. You could just as easily have plotted the number of claims against the amounts claimed to see if there is any relationship between these two variables. In this case, you will see that they tend to increase together.

Graph 8.7 shows such a graph that has been added to the sheet, where the relationship can be seen. Simply plot one variable (X) against another variable (Y). Time does not matter in this case. In practice, such graphs would be used with a much larger amount of data where the relationship might not be so obvious.

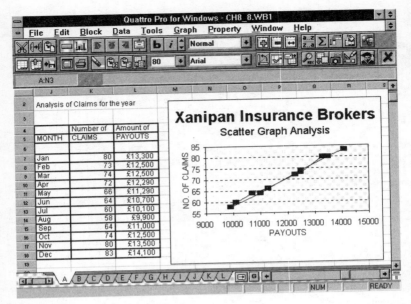

Graph 8.7

It can be seen that when the number of claims is high, so is the amount claimed; demonstrating positive correlation. Another relationship could be the opposite. For example, if you were to plot rainfall against temperature, you might find that on days when rainfall is high, there is a tendency for temperatures to be lower; this is called negative correlation.

● Highlight cells K7..L18.

● Create a new graph as Graph9.

You will see that Quattro Pro makes an instant attempt to determine what the series are and will default to a bar graph.

● Click on OK and examine your graph.

Next you will attempt to alter the graph type to an XY graph.

● Click on Graph, then on Type and then, from the 2-D collection of graphs, click on the XY graph icon.

● Click on OK and see what you are being told.

An XY graph must have an X-axis plotted. Highlighting a block of cells prior to creating a new graph simply speeds up the selection of the Y series. The X Axis series will have to be typed in.

- Click on <u>G</u>raph and then on <u>S</u>eries.

- Delete the second series and type in the block L7..L18 in the X-Axis series instead.

- Now click on OK.

Before moving to the next chapter, try experimenting with this graph to see the effect that changing the data might have.

Try the following:

- Return to the spreadsheet and insert your graph on to the spreadsheet beside the table.

- Create numbers in the table so that as the number of claims increases the amounts claimed decrease.

- Randomise the figures so that there is no apparent correlation.

——— 8.9 Chapter summary ———

This chapter has set out to cover many of the graphics creation aspects of Quattro Pro. The chapter has not covered all aspects and will leave you to investigate other aspects more fully. In this chapter you have:

- Determined X- and Y-axes.

- Set up a simple bar chart.

- Constructed a multiple bar chart.

- Typed in titles and legends to a graph.

- Altered the perspective of graphs.

- Constructed a stack bar chart.

- Constructed pie charts.

- Constructed line graphs with single and multiple variables.

- Constructed three dimensional graphs.

- Altered the scaling of an axis.

- Constructed scatter graphs.

9

ANNOTATING OBJECTS —— AND CREATING —— SLIDE SHOWS

—— 9.1 Aims of this chapter ——

This chapter introduces you to some of the features Quattro Pro has which allow you to develop your own unique graphics and to display them in the form of a slide show.

You will begin the chapter by creating graphic slides using the Graphics Annotation features, adding to the graphs created in the previous chapter developed around the insurance company data.

You will then go on to create a basic slide show that will automatically display a sequence of images from a defined table of data parameters.

The skills developed in this chapter will be useful if you need to use Quattro Pro for presentations, or in shop windows and at exhibitions.

— 9.2 Creating and altering an object —

This first section is designed to give you practice and some suggested 'playing around' time before getting on to creating something developed on the insurance broker created in the last chapter. You will create an object similar to that shown in **Screen dump 9.1** of text in a box that reads 'Quattro Pro for Windows'. The exact likeness you create is not important and may, in any case, be very difficult to achieve. The principle is that you can create and manipulate your own object on a blank graphics screen.

● Start off with a new spreadsheet.

● Click on Graph and then click on New and accept the name Graph1.

● Click on OK from here without typing in any series blocks.

● Now click on the Graph maximise button on the top right of the graph screen (to the right of the title bar that reads NOTEBK1.WB1:graph1) to increase the size of the work area.

At this stage you will be presented with a blank screen.

The Annotate area of the screen consists of the icons on the graph icon bar in the form of shapes. There are ten in all below the pull-down menu options of Data and Tools. In the top right corner of these is a letter A (referred to as the Text icon).

Look at **Screen dump 9.1** again to see what the first object will look like that you are going to create.

● Click on the Text icon (A icon).

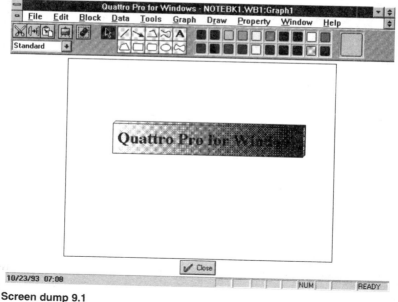

Screen dump 9.1

● Position your mouse pointer somewhere in your graph area and left click your mouse button to confirm the original whereabouts of your object.

● Now place the mouse pointer over the object and click your right mouse button to activate the object inspector for this particular object.

● If you are a version 5.0 user, you will need to click on the text box properties option first.

The object inspector is relevant to this TEXT object only and allows you to make all sorts of alterations to its final outlook before you commit it to appear on your screen.

There are three colour-related options in this object inspector. Use each one for practice. Fill Color will determine the colour of the object where the text will appear.

● Click on Fill Color.

● Click on a light colour such as yellow.

(Background) Bkg Color gives the object a background colour. It can be used, for example, when the object has been given a fill type with a Wash effect (see below).

● Try a dark colour such as dark blue by clicking on Bkg Color and then clicking on the colour.

Border Color colours the rim of the object.

● Click on Border Color and then click on black or a similar dark colour.

The object in Screen dump 9.1 shows the shade of the object altering from left to right. Quattro Pro calls this effect Wash.

● Click on Fill Style from the object inspector and choose the Wash option if you want this effect.

The next stages allow the opportunity to alter the box the text is to be placed in, if any, and how you want the text aligned in the box.

● Now click on Box Type from Box properties and click on the 3-dimensional box.

● Again, from Box properties click on Alignment and make the settings:

Word wrap off (remove the tick)

Centre Align (click on middle icon).

● Click on OK.

The effect of turning the word wrap off is to stop the text from being split across two lines. The centre align places the text in the centre of the object ensuring there is equal room for spaces each side of the text in the object.

● Now type the text Quattro Pro for Windows. Use spaces to give some space both sides of the text in the object.

● Position the mouse pointer in a blank area of the graph and click the left mouse button.

To alter the actual text requires the use of another object inspector related to the text itself.

● Place the mouse pointer over the text itself and then click the right mouse key to activate a different object inspector.

● Click on the Font option in the text property.

The selection of fonts for the object is as comprehensive as those for the spreadsheet, offering you a range of point sizes for each font.

● From here click on Point size and then click on 30. The default is 18 and, consequently, this will increase the size of any text written.

● Placing your mouse pointer somewhere in the blank area of the graph area, click the left button of your mouse to end the editing session on the object.

The object should now be in place on the screen. You can further edit the object, although you should be careful about which object inspector to activate, as there two for text objects. Activating the overall text box object inspector requires the mouse pointer over the edge of the object while the text itself requires the mouse pointer over the text. You can also move the object about in exactly the same way as you have moved blocks of cells in your spreadsheets.

● Placing your mouse pointer over the edge of the object, click your right mouse button to activate the object inspector.

- Experiment with some of the options available in the object inspector to alter its appearance.

- When you are finished return to the graphics screen by clicking your left mouse button while the mouse pointer is over a blank area of your graphs screen.

- Now place the mouse pointer over the edge of the object again and left click your mouse button. With the mouse pointer still over the object, hold the left mouse button down.

A small hand should now appear over the object.

- Moving the mouse slowly, move your object to another position on the screen and release the mouse button.

The annotation facility is very similar to graphic packages available in Windows software in both its jargon and methodology. If you have worked with such packages before you will find much of this quite straightforward and requiring minimal effort on your part. If not, then this is a good time to give yourself plenty of practice. Annotation also lends itself well to the use of the mouse. Without a mouse, you will find producing objects a slow process.

—— 9.3 Creating a variety of objects ——

This next section gives you the opportunity to experiment by creating nine other objects similar to those shown in **Screen dump 9.2.**

- Click on **W**indow from the menu bar and return to your spreadsheet.

- Create another graph, naming it Graph2.

- Maximise the graph area so that you can work more easily.

Observing **Screen dump 9.2** you will see a number of objects that are available. When creating the objects, do not expect to be able to create an exact copy of those in **Screen dump 9.2** as such accuracy is unnecessary. The objects are created using the object icons which work in much the same way as the text object created earlier.

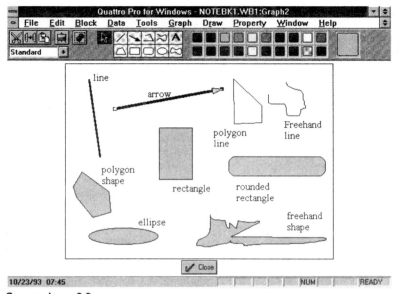

Screen dump 9.2

The line and arrow icon draws a straight line with or without an arrow head. Both work in much the same way.

● Click on the Line icon and position the mouse pointer somewhere in the drawing area.

● Holding down the left mouse button, move the mouse slowly and gently to another position in the drawing area and the other end of line will be dragged. Let go of the button where you want the other end of the line to be and a straight line will be drawn.

● Now repeat this for the Arrow.

● Position the mouse pointer over either object and press the right mouse key to activate the object inspector for the object. Experiment with the options available.

The Polyline and Polygon icons work in exactly the same way as the straight line and arrow icons except that when you double click the left mouse button the last point plotted is joined up with the first point created. The difference between Polyline and Polygon is that the Polygon fills with the chosen Fill Color.

● Create a Polygon as described with any number of sides you choose.

- Click on a colour from the object inspector.

- Repeat this for the Polyline object.

There are two freehand shapes available. Again, one is filled with a colour while the other is not. This works in a similar way to the straight line except that the mouse draws a line as you move it. You will need a fairly steady hand to achieve any degree of accuracy here.

- Experiment with these two freehand objects, altering the properties of the objects with their respective object inspectors.

Finally, there are the three objects of Rectangle, Rounded Rectangle and Ellipse. Drag the shape from the centre in the graph area and then alter the properties as before.

- For each shape click on the respective icon.

- Create the three types of objects in the drawing area and experiment with their properties.

The arrow key below the Block option in the menu bar is the selection tool and is used if you want to leave a particular object.

— 9.4 Moving and deleting objects —

This section examines the facility of moving objects around the screen as well as deleting unwanted ones. First, it may be worth getting a better look at what you have achieved.

- Click on <u>W</u>indow from the menu bar and return to the spreadsheet notebook area.

- Click on <u>G</u>raph, and then on View.

- Click on Graph2.

Viewing the annotated objects is done in exactly the same way as viewing a graph. In fact, in the next section you will be shown how to create objects on top of your graphs.

To delete an object:

- Position the mouse pointer over the object to be deleted and click your left mouse button to make the object the subject.

At this point you should see the edges of the object highlighted with a series of small blocks.

● Press the delete key on your keyboard and the object will disappear.

To move an object:

● Position the mouse pointer over the object to be moved and click your left mouse button.

● Now press your left mouse button again, this time keeping it depressed.

● Move the mouse slowly and the object will be dragged to where you want it.

● When you let go of the mouse button the object will stay where you have dragged it.

You have now been able to create a range of objects, delete them, and move them around the graph drawing area. It is now time to work with the graphs created in the previous chapter.

Exit from your spreadsheet, saving your work if you so wish. If you leave the spreadsheet without this work saved, Quattro Pro will offer you the opportunity to save the work first.

———— 9.5 Preparing slides ————

In this section you will be required to reload the spreadsheet created in the last chapter. The spreadsheet file was called INSURANCE and should now be loaded into your spreadsheet.

To recap on the state of this file you should have a set of named graphs as Graph1, Graph2 . . . to Graph9.

These graphs, in the order in which they appear above, will form the basis of a slide show starting with a new introductory slide that will be an annotation based on the one shown in **Screen dump 9.3**.

The objective is to show each graph, starting with the introduction, as a slide on the screen and displayed for about 15 seconds each.

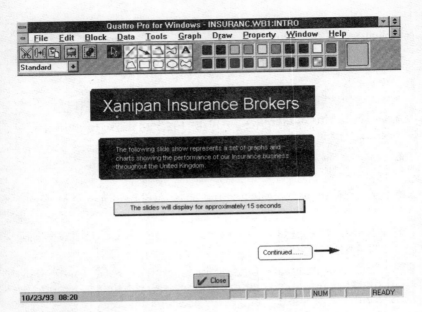

Screen dump 9.3

- Click on <u>F</u>ile from the menu bar and then click on Save <u>A</u>s and save your file with the file name OBJECTS.

- Click on File again and then click on <u>R</u>etrieve to retrieve the spreadsheet.

- Click on the file named as INSURANC, that was developed in the last chapter.

- Make sure your cell pointer is in an empty cell somewhere on your spreadsheet.

- Create a new graph and name it INTRO.

- Create a slide similar to that in **Screen dump 9.3**. An exact copy is, in no way, required. All objects are text objects with alterations made to both the text and box properties.

To create text on more than one line, as appears in **Screen dump 9.3**, you simply press the **Enter** key at the end of a line so that you are able to start the next.

- When you have done this, return to the spreadsheet and use function key **F11** to inspect your first slide.

Apart from creating annotated slides in this way, you can also add objects to graphs through annotation. **Screen dump 9.4** shows such a graph where the objects of a text box with 'More' in it and an arrow object appear in the bottom right corner of the draw area.

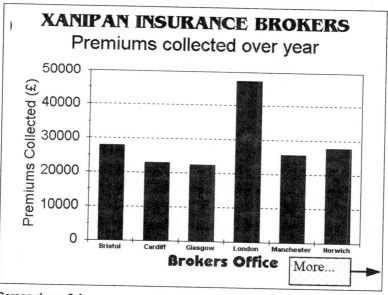

Screen dump 9.4

This was done on the first of the list of named graphs, graph1, and can be done on all named graphs if you so wish. In fact any number of objects can be placed on graphs, although there is an upper limit way beyond most needs. It should now be apparent that all graphs are, in fact, a collection of objects in their own right.

● Click on Graph and then click on Edit and then choose Graph1.

● Using the text icon, create a boxed piece of text with More... in it at the foot of the graph.

● Now use the arrow icon to create an arrow as shown in **Screen dump 9.4**

——— 9.6 Creating a slide show ———

To create a slide show decide:

1 What slides are to make up the show

2 How long each slide is to be shown

3 The visual effect of how the slide is built up

4 How fast the visual effect build-up is to be

Such information is set up as a Light Table of graphs and codes within the graph page. To begin with you will need to get to the graph page, which is the final page on the page identifiers labelled at the foot of your notebook – page IV.

● Click on the Graphics page indicator:

IO	£4,300	£2,300	£1,700	:
IO	£10,500	£4,200	£3,400	:
IO	£4,600	£1,400	£1,100	:
iO	£6,300	£900	£1,300	:
iO	£36,200	£13,500	£10,000	£

H / I / J /   [→] G [←]

If you observe **Screen dump 9.5** you will see the graphs page that should appear. (Three black lines have been superimposed on the screen simply to show you where the three icons are placed that are needed for your slide show.)

The left icon will be used to create your slide show, the middle one will be used to edit the slide show, while the one on the right will be used to run the slide show.

As a starting-point, you will need to create the slide show by indicating which graphs in the list are to be included. In this instance

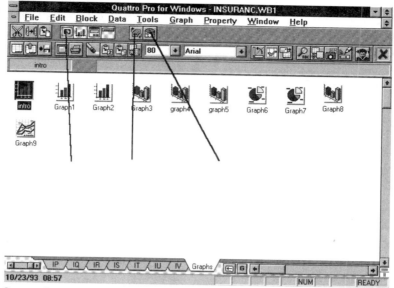

Screen dump 9.5

they will all be included and appear once. There is no reason why some cannot appear more than once or not at all.

● Click your left mouse button on a blank area of the graph page. This ensures no graph is accidentally included in the slide show in the wrong place.

● Now click on Create Slide Show. A dialogue box will appear.

● Type in the name Xanipan, which will become the name of your slide show. Click on OK and an additional icon will appear on your graph page.

At this stage you have defined a slide show but with no slides in it.

The next stage will be to add slides to the show and state how you want them to appear on your screen.

● Position your mouse pointer over the INTRO icon which repre-sents the introduction page of objects you created earlier.

● Hold down your left mouse button and slowly drag the icon and position it on top of the newly created slide show icon.

● Let go of your mouse button and the INTRO icon will reappear back where you dragged it from.

This has placed the first graph into the slide show.

● Repeat this process for all other graph icons placing them, in turn, into the slide show.

At this stage you will have a collection of graphs making up your slide show. You are now in a position to see, and check for your self, whether the slide show is complete.

● Click on the Run Slide Show from the speedbar.

Each graph will show on your screen giving you an idea of what makes up the slide show and how it works.

● Use your Return key to move to the next slide.

You can terminate the slide show at any time by pressing the **Esc** (Escape) key on your keyboard.

● When you have ended the slide show, click on the Edit Slide show icon on the speedbar of your graph page and then click on the 'Xanipan' slide show listed.

A Light Table will appear in a few moments with each of the slides showing. At this stage you are able to make a whole series of changes. By highlighting and dragging, you are able to move the slides around to alter the order in which they appear in your show. You can also alter, for each slide, the way in which it appears on the screen. Observe **Screen dump 9.6** to see an image of the second slide being altered.

● Highlight a slide image by placing your mouse pointer over it and left clicking the mouse button followed by a right click.

Screen dump 9.6 shows the list of effects that are available. This is activated by clicking the mouse left button over the down arrow next to the Effect box which has, as a default, Cut in it. You can alter the time it is displayed on the screen as well as the speed (Slow, Medium, Fast) the next slide appears on the screen. Activating the overlay will place the graph over the previous one.

● Go through each of the graphs in the Light Table altering the way graphs appear on the screen and keeping each graph on the screen for 15 seconds.

● When you have finished click on OK to return to the graph page.

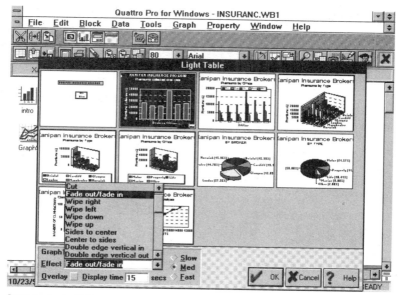

Screen dump 9.6

● Return to Page 'A' where your spreadsheet appears by clicking on the page indicator at the foot of your spreadsheet. A small slide appears to the left of the page indicators that can be used to reveal the pages at the lower end of the alphabet.

● Click on the Graph option from the menu bar.

● Click on Slide Show, and then from the list of slide shows click on Xanipan, followed by OK.

You can, of course, create more than one slide show with the same graphs appearing differently and in a different order. Such slide shows can be useful for exhibitions, displays or presentations.

The next section of this chapter will show you how you can leave the operator in control of what appears on the screen by way of graphs.

——— 9.7 Creating graph buttons ———

It is possible to allow a user to work through the slides in any order they wish and at their own pace. This is particularly useful if they are using this facility to deliver a presentation.

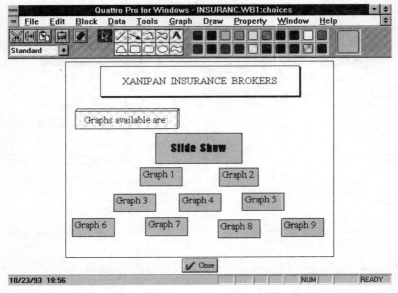

Screen dump 9.7

Observe **Screen dump 9.7** to see a screen of annotated text objects which has been viewed from the spreadsheet. Associated with many of the objects is a graph that can be selected. This is done by placing the mouse pointer over the object, such as Graph 1, clicking the left mouse button and the graph appears for a specified time before returning to the screen. The slide show box will show all slides as shown earlier. The method of achieving this is not a great deal different from creating a macro button as shown in Chapter 7.

● Ensure you have the cell pointer in a blank area of your spreadsheet and click on Graph from the menu bar.

● Click on <u>N</u>ew to create a new graph and name it Choices.

● Now create the objects similar to those that appear in **Screen dump 9.7**. Again, an exact likeness is not important. In this instance it is simply good enough to have a text object associated with each graph and one for the slide show.

● Now activate the object inspector with your right mouse button for one of the graph boxes, making sure it is not the text object inspector for that object.

● If you are a version 5.0 user, you will need to click on Text Box Properties first.

At this stage you have an object inspector where the top option on the list of options down the left is Graph Button. It should default to this leaving you with two choices: Select Graph and Execute Macro.

● Click on the Select Graph box.

● Now click on the graph you want activated with that text box from the list of graphs available.

You will now be able to determine both the effect the graph appears on the screen as well as the time it appears on the screen. **Screen dump 9.8** illustrates such a setting.

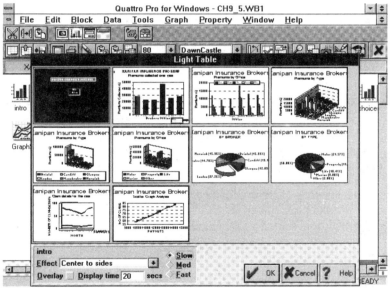

Screen dump 9.8

The settings have been set to show Graph1 for 20 seconds and to appear after a slow interval.

● Make the required setting from the options available and then click on OK to return to your graph edit window.

You will not be able to test the graph button while you are in the edit mode. Instead you will have to view the graph and test it while the graph appears full-screen.

- Press function key **F11** to see the graph called 'Choices' in full view.

- Placing your mouse pointer over the text box against which you set the graph, click your left mouse button.

- Return to the Graph Edit mode and create the required graph buttons for each of the remaining graphs.

In practice, you ought to put some real meaning against each graph button by possibly typing text into each box that gives a better idea of what the graph is going to show.

You can also create a graph button that activates a macro. In this instance you create a graph button that first runs your slide show and then a graph button that prints out your tables.

- Right click your mouse over the text box that will act as the graph button for your slide show.

- If you are a version 5.0 user, you will have to click on Text Box Properties

- From the Graph Button option click on Execute Macro.

At this point you can type in a macro name that has already been created and named somewhere on your spreadsheet. In this instance, you will run a slide show called Xanipan that has already been set up in this chapter.

- Type in {Slide.Run "Xanipan"} noting the use of curly brackets and a full stop.

- Click on OK.

- Press function key **F11** to see the graph full screen.

- Now left click while pointing at the appropriate text box for your slide show.

You can stop your slide show by pressing the **Esc** key on your keyboard at any time.

At this stage you now have a screen of graph buttons for displaying graphs and running a slide show. As another illustration, you will now create two macros for printing the two respective parts of the spreadsheet. To do this the macros can either be recorded using the Macro Record option in the Tools pull-down menu or written down as appears in **Screen dump 9.9**. As suggested in Chapter 7, recording the movements of your actions is always the easier way if you have no instructions to go by. At this stage you will need to return to your spreadsheet in order to prepare and name your two macros.

● Return to your spreadsheet notebook area.

● Click on the Tools option from the menu bar and from here click on Macro.

● Now click on Record.

● Type in A150 as the cell where the macro is to be recorded and then click on OK.

● Press your **Home** key to return to cell A1.

● Now highlight cells A1 to H16.

● Click on File from the menu bar and then click on Print.

● Click on the printer icon to start the printing.

Once the printing has stopped you are then able to finish the macro record and name it. From here, you can then create a graph button to activate it. **Screen dump 9.9** shows the macro that has been recorded and subsequently written in from cell A150 to A152.

● Click on Tools from the menu bar and then click on Macro.

● Click on Stop Record to stop the macro recording process.

● Now go to cell A150 and name block A150 to A152 as the macro P1.

● Create a macro starting at cell D150 that creates the other printing macro and name this P2. You can either record the macro as you did before or copy the other macro, altering the spreadsheet co-ordinates that are to be printed as the block J1 to P20.

Now to create the graph buttons.

● Click on Graph, then on Edit and click on the graph named Choices.

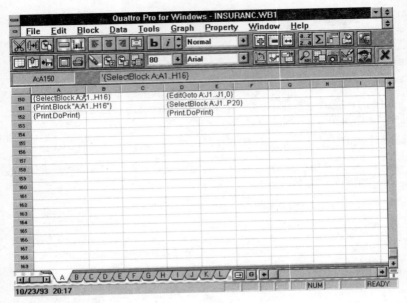

Screen dump 9.9

● Create two new text boxes, one for

> Print Table of
> Premiums Collect

and the other for

> Print Table of
> Claims Analysis.

● Now activate the text box object inspector for each, and click on the Execute Macro box from the graph button option.

● Against each Execute Macro, type in the name of the macro associated with each graph button as either P1 or P2.

When typing in the macro, ensure that the macro names of P1 and P2 are both placed between the curly brackets.

● Return to your spreadsheet and use function key **F11** to view the Choices graph.

● Experiment with each graph button that uses the two printing macros to make sure they actually work.

As a finishing touch to this spreadsheet create the following macro buttons similar to those set up in Chapter 7, remembering that they are macro buttons stored on the spreadsheet rather than graph buttons. The macro button is created using the respective icon on the speedbar.

● Macros to create:

1 To go to the Analysis of Claims table that starts at cell location J1.

2 To view the graph (Graph View) of choices where the graph buttons are stored.

3 To run a slide show from the spreadsheet.

4 To print either part of the spreadsheet.

As you already have P1 and P2 set up, you need only create the two macro buttons and use them. Place each macro button beside each table and call them: 'Print Table'.

——— 9.8 Chapter summary ———

This chapter has only given a brief overview of what is possible with the annotation of objects. Quattro Pro offers many more facilities that can be easily developed with what has been shown in this chapter.

Many of the built-in help facilities of Quattro Pro can help you, as can the User's Guide that comes with the package.

In this chapter you have:

● Annotated and created a variety of objects.

● Altered the properties of objects.

● Moved and deleted objects.

● Set up an automatic slide show.

● Set up a slide show for user control.

● Created graph buttons allowing user choice.

● Further developed the creation of macros by recording keyboard commands.

● Created a number of macros and included them as graph button options.

10

THREE-DIMENSIONAL SPREADSHEETS

────── ## 10.1 Aims of this chapter ──────

This chapter will introduce you to the idea of working with multiple spreadsheets. Quattro Pro refers to the concept as three-dimensional.

The principle is that a spreadsheet has columns and rows and so is two-dimensional. A third dimension is added when you have a stack of pages one on top of another. Quattro Pro will allow you to have 256 such pages, although filling all these up will be restricted by the amount of available memory. The idea works rather like a book, in that a single page of the book reads across and down, while a whole series of pages make up a book. Each layer will be called a page, and can be given a reference such as a month name, while the collection of these pages will be called the spreadsheet.

In earlier chapters you have come across the idea of having more than one spreadsheet open at any one time. You can cascade the display of spreadsheets to create a layered effect similar to what you will see in this chapter. The difference, however, is that each page in a three-dimensional spreadsheet is permanently connected and all load when the spreadsheet is opened. It will also be considerably easier to have linked formulae in one page with data stored on another.

As a final part to this chapter, you will look at a fourth dimension where, in addition to a spreadsheet made up of multiple pages, you can have multiple spreadsheets open at any one time with formulae linking them.

— 10.2 Preparing for multiple pages —

● Start with a new spreadsheet.

At this opening stage you see the tabs of ten pages on your screen named A, B, C to J. The one in the front is labelled page 'A' and is the only visible page in the spreadsheet. In this chapter you will work with four pages to show you how Quattro Pro uses this three-dimensional environment.

As a starting-point, you will name the first three spreadsheets as January, February, March instead of A, B, C.

● Place your mouse pointer on the A indicator at the bottom of the notebook page and click your right mouse button to activate the page object inspector.

● In the Page Name box that appears for page A, type in the name January as a replacement for A and then click on OK.

This page has now been named as January instead of A. If you look at the cell indicator in the Input line you will see that it refers to the cell location with the January prefix.

● Now click the left button of your mouse with the pointer over the B page indicator.

At this stage you will notice that page B becomes the active page.

● Now right click on the page B indicator to reveal the page object inspector again and give the page the name February.

● Repeat this for page C giving it the name March.

● Return to the February page by clicking your left mouse button while the pointer is positioned over the page indicator labelled as February.

● Click on cell C9 on this page.

You can also return to the page by using the **F5** function key and typing in the page reference as February:C9 (cell location C9 on page February). **Screen dump 10.1** shows the pages numbered with February as the active page.

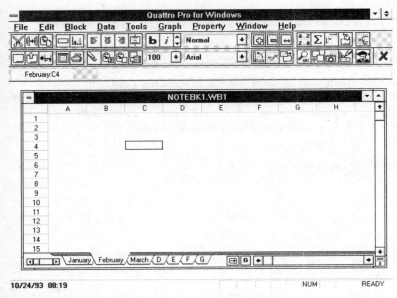

Screen dump 10.1

Although you have selected three pages you will see later in this chapter that you can always add or delete pages to and from these and place them or delete them before, after and between other pages, rather like a adding or removing pages in a loose-leaf book.

● Use your **F5** function key to go to cell January:A1.

At this stage you should be positioned on the January page. As part of the preparation stages you will group the months in a rather similar way to giving a block of cells a name. The purpose of this will be to allow you to format a whole group of pages in one set of actions rather than format each page individually. You will first need to define the group and then activate the Group mode.

● Click on the **T**ools option from the menu bar then click on Define **G**roup.

Observe **Screen dump 10.2** to see how the group has been defined.

Pages January to March have been given Group Name Months. It is rather like grouping a block of pages in a book and calling it a chapter with a chapter name.

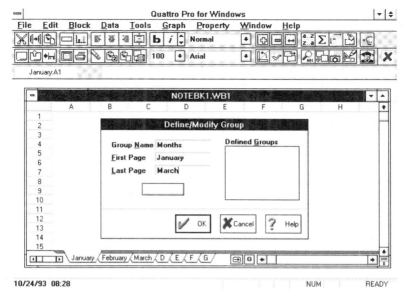

Screen dump 10.2

● Type in the settings in Screen dump 10.2 and then click on OK.

● Now click on the G button at the bottom of your notebook area which lies to the right of the page indicator tabs.

A small blue line will now appear below the three months of January to March to indicate that the three pages form the one group.

—— 10.3 Setting up the first page ——

This example will begin by setting up the January page with a Sales Analysis table for Europa Components to different companies in the month of January.

● Ensure that the current working Page is January.

● As a first measure, widen column A to about twice its current width.

● Now look at the February page and then March.

You will observe that the other pages on the Months group have also been altered accordingly. This is simply because the Group button (G) has been activated. Any pages outside this group will not have been altered.

● Return to the January page.

● Type in the labels:

In cell	type
A1	EUROPA COMPONENTS
A3	Sales Analysis by Country
D3	JANUARY
A5	Country
B5	Sales
B6	Value
C5	Percentage

● Type in the 9 countries in the block of cells from A8 to A16, as they appear in **Screen dump 10.3**.

● Widen columns B and C to about twice their current width.

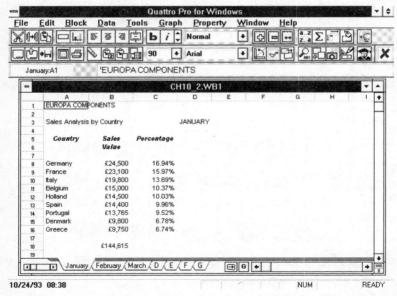

Screen dump 10.3

● To make the headings more presentable, highlight the cells B5 to D6 and, from the notebook object inspector, select the Alignment option and centre the text.

● With the block still highlighted set fonts in bold and in italics by clicking on the two speedbar icons labelled B and I.

● Type in a set of sales values in the block B8 to B16, as in Screen dump 10.3.

At this point there is no longer a need to have the Group mode on. Any alterations to the spreadsheet will not be necessary just yet and you will need the Group mode off so that you can type in formulae specific to a particular page.

● Switch the Group mode off by clicking on the Group button.

● Highlight the cells B8 to B16, click on Block, then Names, then Create and name the block as January:SALES.

Note that the page reference has been used. The reason for this will become apparent later when setting up the February sales figures.

● Now type in the function @SUM(SALES) in cell B18.

● Format, from the notebook object inspector, the block of cells B8..B18 as currency and to zero decimal places.

● Type in the formula +B8/B$18 in cell C8. Note how the row reference of 18 in the formula has been fixed as absolute. This will permit copying.

● Now format this cell using the notebook object inspector to percentage and to two decimal places.

● Copy the formula in cell C8 to the block of cells C9 to C16.

Observe **Screen dump 10.3** to make sure that you have the similar set-up.

—— 10.4 Copying between pages ——

Your next objective will be to copy the entire contents of January to February. The principle of doing this is no different from copying from a block of cells to another on the same page.

- Remove Group mode.
- Highlight all the cells in the block A1 to C18.
- Copy the block to the clipboard.
- Position your mouse pointer in February and at cell A1.
- Now Paste the clipboard contents to this location.
- Switch Group mode back on.

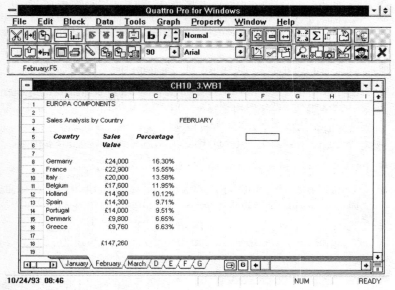

Screen dump 10.4

You now have an identical copy of the pages in both parts of the spreadsheet.

A whole host of options is copied in one stroke, including style options.

- Type in a new set of sales figures for February as appears in **Screen dump 10.4**.

- Amend the month in cell D3 to FEBRUARY.

As the new figures are typed in, so the sum in cell B18 and the percentages in column C will alter as well.

— 10.5 Typing in three-dimensional — formulae

You will now type into February a formula that works out the difference between sales in the current month of February with those of the previous month of January. In other words, the differences of the values in the respective B6 cells.

● With Group mode on, widen column D.

Because the Group mode is on it will automatically set the column widths for all pages in the group.

● Switch the Group mode off.

● Type in the new column heading Sales Change in D5 and on Month in D6. Centre align all heading labels and set them in bold and italic using the speedbar icons.

Now you are ready to use a formula that links with the other page.

● In cell D8 type in the formula +B8–January:B8.

Cell B8 contains the monthly sales for Germany in the current page for February. Cell January:B8 is in the January page as its prefix implies, and contains the German sales for January. The formula calculates the difference in sales between the two months. A negative figure would imply a fall in sales between the two months; a positive figure implies an increase.

Now you need to do the same for the remaining countries. Because the relative position of the remaining countries all remain the same, you will be able to copy and paste the formula already typed in to the remaining countries.

● Click on cell D8, click on Edit from the menu bar and then click on Copy.

● Now highlight the block of cells D9 to D16 and Paste the clipboard contents to the block.

● Now copy totalling function in cell B18 to D18.

● Set the block of numbers D8..D18 to currency and to zero decimal places.

● Now switch the Group mode back on in preparation for some alterations in the presentation.

Examine **Screen dump 10.5**.

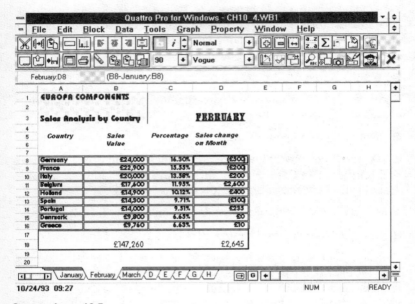

Screen dump 10.5

● Change the Style of February as though it was the only page in use. Do not be too concerned at getting an exact likeness.

● Now hop between January and February to see the effect.

Observe how the page settings have been created across both months.

● Now hop to March to see how the screen presentation is ready for the cell entries.

Any page outside of the group will not have been altered. You will find it worth looking to confirm this.

——— 10.6 Building up a history ———

The next stage is to copy the contents of February to March to give sales for March.

● Switch the Group mode off for now and make sure you are on the February page.

● Highlight the entire page of February starting at cell A1 and copy the block to the clipboard.

● Go to cell A1 in March and paste the clipboard contents to this position.

● In cell D3 change February to March.

Screen dump 10.6 shows the likely result with the screen presentation all done for you as well.

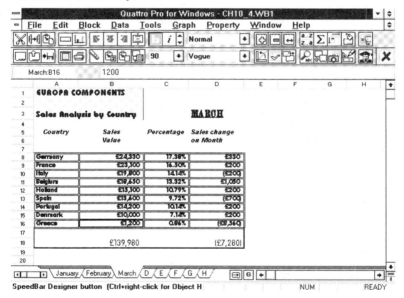

Screen dump 10.6

At first you will notice that the Sales change on month columns shows all zeros. This is exactly to be expected because as both monthly figures in February and March are at present the same, their differences will be zero. This would confirm that the formulae have been copied successfully as well as the numbers and labels.

● Using the data in Screen dump 10.6, amend the monthly sales figures for the countries and observe what happens to the figures in the column Sales Changes on month as you work through it.

You should now be able to appreciate that the task becomes easier as you work through the months. You may, for example, want to go on with this for many more months.

—— 10.7 Summarising the pages ——

The next task is to produce a summary page that adds all the monthly sales figures together. You could type this, say, as page Z, giving yourself room for many more months after March. However, this is unnecessary as you will always have the opportunity to insert pages between existing ones in the same way as you would insert a new column or row within a single page.

Screen dump 10.7 shows the desired effect where the Sales Value figures are the totals for each of the three months you have already typed in on pages January, February and March.

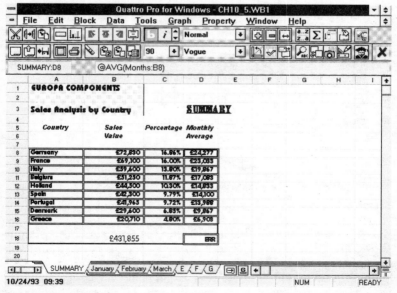

Screen dump 10.7

The figures in column B will add up all monthly sales from January to March and column D will calculate the average sales for each country over the three months. In both cases, the formulae will be calculated on figures across more than one page.

First you will insert a page at the front of the spreadsheet so that the summary sheet is in the same place as January with the other months all pushed back one place.

● Go to the January page and ensure that Group mode is off.

● Click on Block from the menu bar and then click on Insert.

● Now click on the Pages option.

● Click on OK to insert the new page.

If you had left the Group mode on, the page insertion would have inserted three pages as Quattro Pro would assume you wanted a new group of pages equivalent to the Months group that you named earlier.

● Copy the entire contents of the January page to the A page.

● Now turn the Group mode back on.

As this new page is not part of the group, the column widths are different from the Months group.

● Widen the columns.

● Amend the label in D3 to read SUMMARY.

● Using the Page object inspector, name the page Summary.

● Amend the label in D5 to 'Monthly' and D6 to 'Sales'.

● Highlight cells B8 to B16 and press the **delete** key on your keyboard.

● Click on cell B8 and type in the formula @SUM(Months:B8).

● Copy the function in B8 to the block B9 to B16.

The function in cell B8 has added together the contents of the three values in B8 for the pages January to March in a three-dimensional sense. It would now be easy to add another page for another month for April and then include this extra month in the group by renaming the group as Months to include April.

As a further demonstration of how the three-dimensional effect works, you will calculate a formula that works out the average monthly sales value of the three months' sales value figures.

● Click on cell D8 and type in the function @AVG(Months:B8) and then copy this formula from cell D8 to the block of cells D9 to D16.

You now have two sets of formulae that make use of the three-dimensional effect. If you are unsure as to what has happened, then browse through the block of cells where the formulae have been set to see how it has worked.

In order to gain a better appreciation of how this works, you will now create a set of figures for April on page D.

● Copy the contents of March to page D and name this page March.

● Type in a set of figures for the sales values using the data in **Screen dump 10.8**.

● Switch the Group mode off.

● Click on <u>B</u>lock from the menu bar and then click on <u>N</u>ames. Delete the Months group name and <u>C</u>reate a group name of Months from January to April.

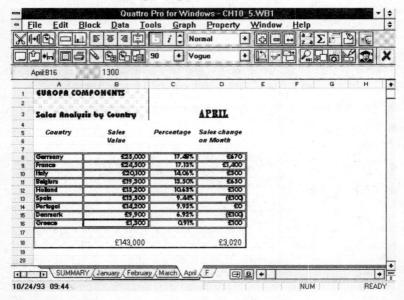

Screen dump 10.8

- Now switch the Group mode back on and have a look at the Summary page again to see the effect.

— 10.8 Adding a fourth dimension —

This chapter has covered the idea of multiple pages for the four different months. After one year has elapsed, the whole process really ought to start again. In this instance you would create another page on the lines of what has already been achieved. To do this easily, you could create a new spreadsheet and Copy the previous year's pages into it.

Instead of simply saving the existing spreadsheet with a new name, this final demonstration will show you how you can use the copy command to duplicate the four pages from one worksheet to another. In effect, you will have a fourth dimension by having more than one multiple paged spreadsheet open at the same time.

The rest of this chapter now assumes that you have added a new month of April to give you five pages of summary and January to April.

- Click on File from the menu bar and then click on Save As and save the spreadsheet as Year1.

- Again, click on File and then click on Save As and save the spreadsheet as Year2.

You will now have two files, Year1 and Year2 of which Year2 is the current spreadsheet in use.

- Now go through each of the months January to March amending the sales figures. **Screen dump 10.9** shows a set of figures for the new January.

- Ensure the Group mode is switched on.

- Click back to January and type in the label Change in cell E5 and Year in cell E6.

- Complete the formats of this new column so that the headings are in a similar style to the others and the currency has the correct format. You will also need to widen the column.

● Now switch the Group mode off.

● Click on cell E8 in the January page.

The formula in cell E8 needs to subtract the sales value in cell B8 from the corresponding cell in the YEAR1 file. In other words it will be the value of cell January:B8 in YEAR1 spreadsheet less the value of B8 in the current spreadsheet and page. Placing the file name in front of the cell reference and embedding it with square brackets, [ ], will have the desired effect.

● Type in the formula +[YEAR1.WB1]January:B8–B8 in cell E8.

● Now copy this formula from cell E8 to the block E9..E16.

Observe **Screen dump 10.9** to see what the effect should be.

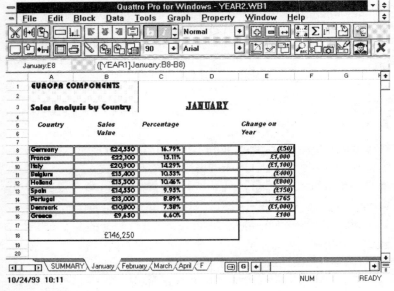

Screen dump 10.9

The power of this should now be clear to see, where you can even copy the formula. Your reference areas of other spreadsheets, in most instances, will be preserved when copying.

● Highlight cells E5..E16 and copy them to cell E5 in February.

● Click on cell E5 in March and again paste the formulae.

You will observe that even here the relative position of the cells in the other spreadsheet is reflected in the formulae you copy. In other words, the February and March figures are worked out as the differences with February and March of the pages in the other spreadsheet.

● Paste this block into April and then save the current spreadsheet as Year2.

——— 10.9 Chapter summary ———

In this chapter you have concentrated on creating and manipulating a three-dimensional spreadsheet. However, this has the advantage of leaving you with only one spreadsheet to concern yourself with in terms of file handling and presents you with easier formulae when working in three dimensions.

You have:

● Created extra pages in a spreadsheet to create a three-dimensional effect.

● Viewed and moved between multiple pages.

● Set up the Group mode and performed Style set ups for all sheets.

● Typed data into one page and copied it to another.

● Typed formulae and functions into a page that are derived from data in other pages.

● Opened another spreadsheet and worked with two multiple-sheet spreadsheets.

● Linked spreadsheets with the [ ] facility.

11

– SAMPLE EXERCISES –

—— 11.1 Aims of this chapter ——

This book has introduced you to a large variety of applications of spreadsheets. This chapter offers further ideas for spreadsheet use.

In addition, some exercises will help develop your skills further with Quattro Pro for Windows. If you work through the exercises in sequence, you will find that they are graded in such a way that they become more demanding as you work through them.

—— 11.2 Selling soft toys ——

1 Load your spreadsheet and type in the spreadsheet title EXPENSE DETAILS FOR HARRY'S SOFT TOYS on the first row. On the third row type in the author's name (your name) along with the date it was generated.

2 Generating today's date requires the @TODAY function followed by formatting the cell. (The date formats are available in the block properties of the object inspector as Numeric Format).

3 Type in rows 6 to 11, as shown in **Screen dump 11.2.**

4 In cell A13, type in the label TOTAL. (Right justify this by typing "TOTAL.)

5 Now type in a formula in cell B13 that calculates the sum of values in the block B7 to B11.

6 Copy the formula from cell B13 to cells C13 to E13.

7 In columns F and G type in data for MAY and JUNE:

	May	June
Wages	455	495
Rent	80	80
Rates	190	190
Heating	15	18
Sundries	26	33

8 In column H type in a column heading: TOTAL.

9 In cell H7 type in a formula that totals the expenses for each category and copy this formula from H7 to the block H8 to H11.

10 Copy the formula in cell E13 to cells F13 to H13.

11 Incorrect information has been collected on the costs of sundries which should be 20 in February and 25 in April. Adjust the amounts accordingly to recalculate the total costs.

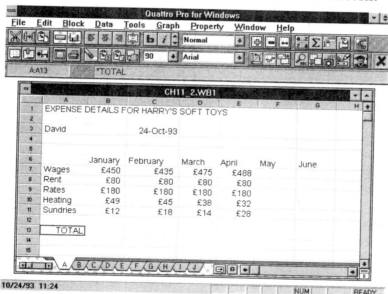

Screen dump 11.2

12 Format all numeric cells so that they are displayed in currency format to zero places of decimals.

13 Add a new row at row 15 and in cell A15 type in the title

INCOME followed by, for each month, the following sales income values:

	Jan	Feb	Mar	Apr	May	Jun
Sales Income	2,000	3,000	3,000	4,000	5,000	5,000

14 Now add a final row called SURPLUS and under the Jan column type in a formula that shows the surplus value as being: (Sales Income) minus (Total Cost). Copy this formula across the spreadsheet.

15 Check that all numeric formats are in currency and make any adjustments to tidy up the presentation.

16 Experiment with some of the fonts to improve the style of your spreadsheet.

17 Print the entire spreadsheet, remembering to define the block you want printed first.

18 Save your work under the filename HARRY.

11.3 Arnold's fish bar

1 Load your spreadsheet and type in your name and today's date at the top of the spreadsheet. Remember, the @TODAY function can be used for this, as described in Chapter 6.

2 Type in a title on row 3: ARNOLD'S FISH BAR SALES.

3 Widen column A.

4 Set up the spreadsheet with the labels shown in **Screen dump 11.3a** with the column headings starting on row 5 and the row headings in column A.

5 The numbers that appear in the spreadsheet should also be typed in. Make sure the text is left-justified and numbers are right-justified.

6 Generate the INCOME obtained from COD by multiplying the PRICE by the number SOLD, putting the answer in the INCOME column.

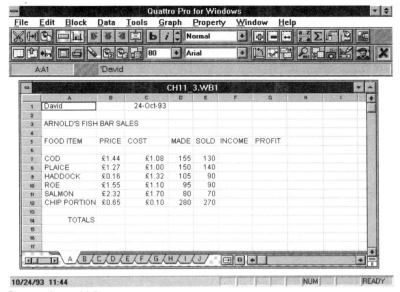

Screen dump 11.3a

7 On row 14 use a formula to calculate the total items MADE, the total dishes SOLD, and the total INCOME.

8 Add an extra column to the spreadsheet to show the profit made on each dish. Under the heading PROFIT generate the data for each dish using the formula:

PROFIT = INCOME – (COST * MADE)

9 Format all money values currency.

10 Now change the numeric data to the ones shown in **Screen dump 11.3b** to check that your spreadsheet still calculates the INCOME, PROFIT and TOTALS correctly with the new figures.

11 Produce two more columns with the column headings UNSOLD to hold the column of stock for each item that was left unsold (MADE – SOLD) and a column headed WASTE to hold the cost to the fish bar of this unsold stock (UNSOLD * COST).

12 Narrow the column widths so that all data are in view on your screen and then compare the outcome with that shown in **Screen dump 11.3b**.

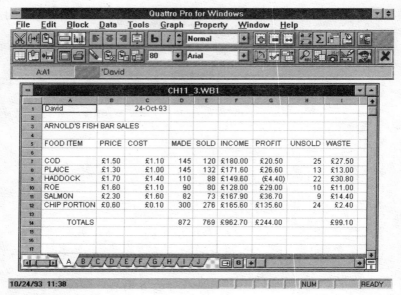

Screen dump 11.3b

13 Make any alterations to the presentation required and save your spreadsheet.

14 Print out this spreadsheet.

11.4 An electricity bill

This exercise requires you to set up a model electricity bill similar to that shown in **Screen dump 11.4**. If you have an electricity bill of your own to use, then model it around this instead.

When you set out this spreadsheet, bear in mind the following formulae:

● No. of units = (Current meter reading) – (Last meter reading)

● Total Cost of units = (No. of Units) * (Cost per Unit) / 100

● VAT = (VAT Rate) * (Total Cost of units + Standing Charge)

● TOTAL NOW DUE = (Total Cost of Units) + (Standing Charge) + VAT

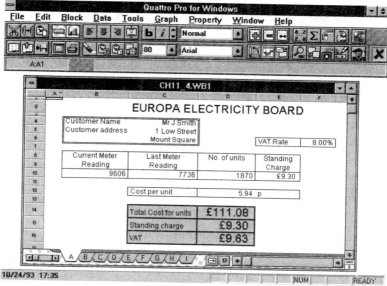

Screen dump 11.4

When you complete the exercise, experiment with a few bills with different meter readings to convince yourself that the spreadsheet works correctly.

11.5 Calorie control

The following exercise is an example of how a spreadsheet can be used to give instant and accurate measures of the number of calories contained within a specific diet. When working through it you ought to consider how it can be extended to include other variables such as certain vitamins.

The spreadsheet is split into two parts: one part contains the ACTUAL DIET of a given patient, while the second part contains the CALORIE CONTROL CHART. Basically, the spreadsheet will collect the details of the patient from a user and then calculate the calories consumed in the diet by reading these details from the Calorie Control Chart.

Calorie control chart

The chart will go on to Page B named as 'Control_Chart'. The data on this page will be standard and do not need to be changed too often.

1 Start at cell position A1 of Page B and type in the details as shown in **Screen dump 11.5a** which will hold the calorie content per 100 grams of a range of food and drink.

When naming a page you are not able to include spaces in the name; hence the use of the small underscore (_) symbol in the title.

2 Name the page accordingly but do not create a group with this page in it because the layout of the screen will be different.

When generating this table, you will need to adjust the column widths to fit the data.

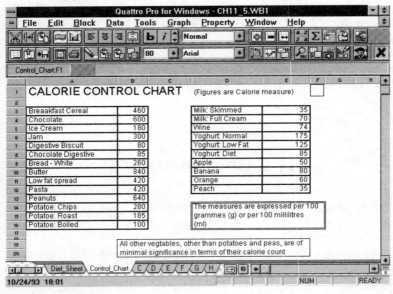

Screen dump 11.5a

3 Change the look of the page with the Line Drawing, Fonts, and Shading facilities within the notebook object inspector. The grid lines can be hidden by using the option in the Page object inspector.

4 Print out the chart. (You will need to specify the block you want printed prior to its actual printing.)

Patient diet page

5 Type in a patient diet page for a given day, starting at cell position A1 on the front page, something like that set out in **Screen dumps 11.5b and 11.5c**. You will observe that the spreadsheet exceeds the number of lines in one screen.

6 Name the page Diet_Sheet.

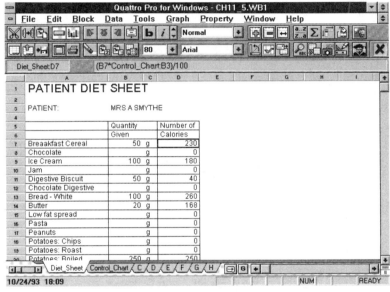

Screen dump 11.5b

7 Be careful to create a column C for the unit of measure (g or ml) and narrow the column. Only the number can go into the amounts given in column C.

8 Make sure that the entries of the NUMBER OF CALORIES are found and calculated by the computer. For example, the number for Full Cream Milk in cell location D22 is calculated as follows: Grams given, to be found in cell B22, divided by 100 and then multiplied by the number of calories per 100 millilitres which was placed into cell E4 of the Diet_Sheet page.

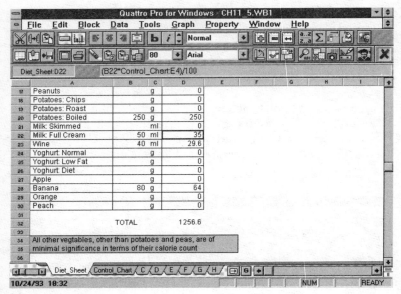

Screen dump 11.5c

Consequently, for cell D22 the formula will need to read
+B22*Control_Chart:E4/100.

9 Perform some of the finishing touches to improve the presentation of your work.

10 Finally, use the @SUM function to find the totals for this patient, then print the details of the patient's diet.

———— 11.6 Employee sickness ————

This exercise requires you to perform the following tasks:

1 Ensure you have started with a blank spreadsheet.

2 Type in a heading and a list of employee names, as shown in **Screen dump 11.6**.

3 Type in for each employee: the number of days sickness and the number of possible days they could have worked.

4 Type in dates From and To using the @DATE function.

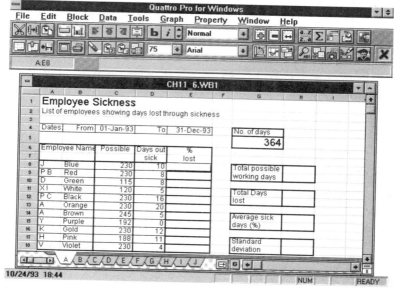

Screen dump 11.6

5 Calculate the number of days between the two dates.

6 Calculate the percentage of days lost through sickness for each employee.

7 Now create NAME blocks of: possible, days lost, and percentage for columns B, C, and D respectively. Make up a table of the named blocks, placing it beneath the table.

8 Calculate total working days, total lost days, an average percentage of days' sickness and a standard deviation for sickness days.

Note: In order to tackle this you will need to know that Quattro Pro has an in-built function for the standard deviation:

@STD(percentage)

9 Smarten up the presentation.

10 Get a printout of the table you have generated.

11 Alter some of the sickday figures and possible workdays to make sure that the calculations work. Print out a second spreadsheet.

—— 11.7 Price lists for a transport —— company

Examine Screen dump 11.7 showing a transport company's price list, before starting this exercise.

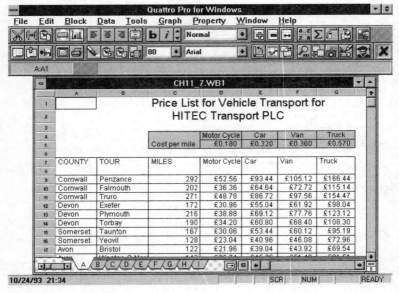

Screen dump 11.7

From observation you will see that there is a heading for a county, and a town or city within that county. The mileage indicates the number of miles from the town to a fictitious London office.

The costs indicate the cost per mile for running each vehicle type. For each town, therefore, the cost of running a vehicle from London to the stated town is calculated. The use of such a spreadsheet allows a new price list to be easily and quickly constructed each time the prices per mile change.

1 Construct such a list for England, Scotland, Wales or any other country by having each county (province or state) represented by between two and four of their principal towns or cities. You will need a map of the country with the mileage between the town or city and your chosen central location.

2 For each country, produce two lists with the following costs:

	first list	second list
Motor Cycle:	£0.18	£0.21
Car:	£0.32	£0.34
Van:	£0.36	£0.33
Truck:	£0.57	£0.55

The monetary values should be in currency format.

3 Rearrange your list using the Sort facilities from the Data pull-down menu into County (Province or State) order and, within each county, organised in town or city order.

4 Save what you created in task 3 and produce the list in town order.

5 Repeat task 4 but rearrange the list into order of distance with the furthest distance at the top of the list.

The whole width of the spreadsheet can be made visible on the screen by adjusting the column widths.

——— 11.8 World weather chart ———

This spreadsheet sets out a world weather chart to show the temperature in different locations throughout the world. See **Screen dump 11.8**.

1 Design a spreadsheet to display this information. Include data taken from newspapers. The temperature in Fahrenheit should be found from the temperature in Centigrade using the formula:

Fahrenheit = Centigrade * 1.8 + 32.

2 At the foot of your table, show:

the average temperature

the number of locations

he name of the hottest place

the name of the coldest place.

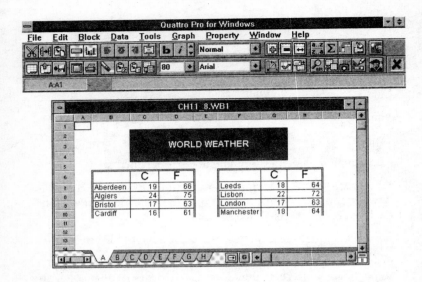

Screen dump 11.8

These figure should be determined using Quattro Pro functions.

3 Print the table.

4 Alter the temperatures.

— 11.9 Car burglar alarm explosion —

This spreadsheet requires you to set out the components of a car burglar alarm system that is to be produced by a small engineering company. The final product will be in black box form ready to install into a car. The objective of this exercise is to calculate, at component level, the cost of materials and production of the alarm in order to derive a profitable selling price.

From the list, shown in **Screen dump 11.9a** and **Screen dump 11.9b**, you should be able to enter the number of alarm systems you wish to make and the spreadsheet will then produce a 'shopping list' giving a list of the components needed and their costs along with a total cost. It is suggested, therefore, that your spreadsheet has the following sections:

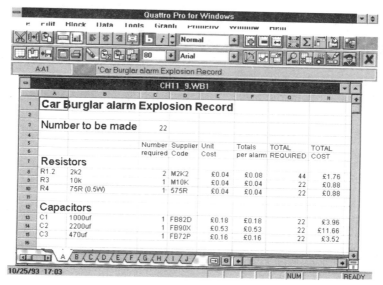

Screen dump 11.9a

● A component breakdown, per alarm, as shown in **Screen dump 11.9a**.

● A column to hold costs of multiple components; for example 10 * 0.4W metal film 2K2.

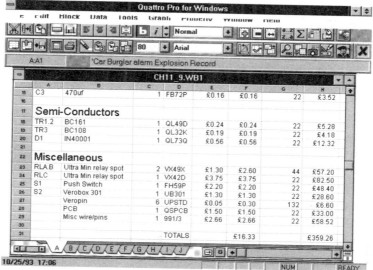

Screen dump 11.9b

- An entry for the desired number of 'final product' car alarm(s).

- A list of total components needed, with unit costs, in alphabetical order.

Try taking advantage of macros in order to sort the list by costs as well as in component order. Also, use a macro to simplify the printing of each section.

You will find the use of a horizontal window useful because the spreadsheet has more rows of information than can be seen on the screen at any one time.

11.10 League tables

This spreadsheet is designed to show a football league championship table and can easily be adapted to suit any league-based sport. The table has been sorted so that the club with the highest number of points appears at the top of the table. When two clubs have the same number of points, the order is by goal difference.

Part of the table takes the form of the one shown in **Screen dump 11.10**.

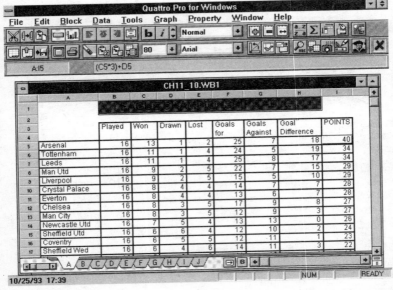

	Played	Won	Drawn	Lost	Goals for	Goals Against	Goal Difference	POINTS
Arsenal	16	13	1	2	25	7	18	40
Tottenham	16	11	1	4	24	5	19	34
Leeds	16	11	1	4	25	8	17	34
Man Utd	16	9	2	5	22	7	15	29
Liverpool	16	9	2	5	15	5	10	29
Crystal Palace	16	8	4	4	14	7	7	28
Everton	16	8	4	4	13	6	7	28
Chelsea	16	8	3	5	17	9	8	27
Man City	16	8	3	5	12	9	3	27
Newcastle Utd	16	7	5	4	13	13	0	26
Sheffield Utd	16	6	6	4	12	10	2	24
Coventry	16	6	5	5	12	11	1	23
Sheffield Wed	16	6	4	6	14	11	3	22

Screen dump 11.10

The points system assumed is:

Win = 3 points

Draw = 1 point

Games Played = Won + Lost + Drawn

Goal Difference = (Goals for) − (Goals against)

1 Produce a spreadsheet for this table or from a league table listed in the sports section of a newspaper.

2 At the foot of the table show the following:

Number of clubs

Highest number of wins

Highest number of defeats

Average number of goals for

Average number of goals against

The average goal difference

All these figures should be shown to the nearest whole figure.

— 11.11 Hayley Computer Services —

This problem involves the setting up of a simple cash budget depicting a cash flow for a company. The pro-forma set out in **Screen dump 11.11** is designed to help you get started with the problem.

Hayley Computer Services Ltd is a small company offering computer consultancy and professional training to small businesses. The company has been trading for two years, the only staff being Mr James and his wife. Mr James is now worried that the £5,000 overdraft facility granted by his bank will be insufficient to finance his company's modest expansion. To assist in his investigation of several possible plans, he has decided to set up a cash flow model covering the next 12 months.

Mrs James has made the following estimates for the year ending December 31.

● Fees received by the company in January will be £2,900 and these will rise steadily by 5% per month.

Expenses of the company are expected to be:

● Rental of premises at £400 per month and have been fixed at this amount for the year.

● General expenses of £500 in January, rising steadily by 3% a month.

● Fixed motor vehicle expenses of £120 per month.

● Wages and tax deductions of £1,800 a month, fixed for 6 months, but increased from July onwards by 25%.

In March Mr James intends changing his company car. He believes that he will be able to sell his present car for £5,600 and that the replacement will cost £7,900.

In September he expects to pay tax of £5,920 on the company's previous year's profits.

On 1 January the company's bank account is expected to be overdrawn by £3,100.

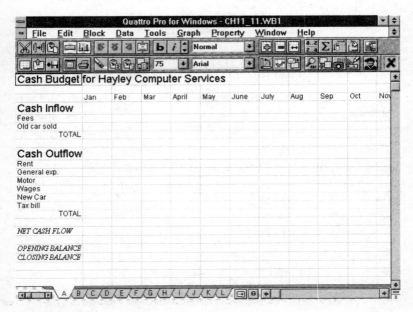

Screen dump 11.11

You are required to:

1 Set up the model of the company's cash flow for the 12 months to December. You have the pro-forma set out in **Screen dump 11.11** to help you get started. All numbers should be displayed to the nearest whole figure.

2 By modifying the basic model, ascertain the effect of each of the following proposals in turn on the company's overdraft position so that Mr James can decide which option most favours his bank balance.

a) A new issue of shares to Mr James' uncle giving a cash inflow of £4,500 in February.

b) Taking out a loan of £4,000 in January to be repaid in December with interest of £450.

c) Deferring the purchase of the new car for 12 months but facing extra running expenses of £40 a month after March.

d) Paying £1,000 for advertising in January with an increase in sales of £250 a month (over and above the 5% growth) beginning in February. Also vacating his rented premises and working at home from January.

— 11.12 The rapid cook microwave — company

This problem requires you to design a cash budget similar to that of exercise 11.11. However, the problems are more demanding and you are given less help with the initial layout.

A group of partners is to set up a limited company for the purpose of manufacturing and selling microwave ovens with start-up Share Capital of £60,000 in the bank on 1 June and an anticipated injection of further Share Capital from new shareholders once the business is under way.

The plans for the company are as follows:

● It will produce 120 ovens a month starting in June but expects sales to start from 60 in July, increasing in steps of 20 each month until they reach 140 per month.

● The ovens will sell for £320 each with customer accounts being settled in the second month after the month of purchase.

● The overheads will be fixed at £5,000 per month paid one month in arrears.

● In September the business will pay £150,000 for machinery and computers needed to start up the business.

● In November, an extra injection of capital is expected. This amount should be £75,000

● The unit (variable) production costs, which are not expected to rise in the period under review, will be as follows:

Materials	£90
Labour	£80
Variable Overheads	£40

Materials will be bought as needed, with payment one month later. Labour will have to be paid in the month in which the expense is incurred as will variable overheads.

● Interest on the previous month's overdraft is to be charged at 1.5% plus a £10 standing charge by the bank.

In order to satisfy the bank manager that the request for additional funding of the business with an overdraft is reasonable, the business has been asked to draw up a cash flow forecast for the first 7 months of operations from June to December.

● Use Quattro Pro to create the cash flow table that the bank manager will want to see before granting the overdraft provision asked for. The cash flow table will also need to show the size of overdraft required.

● You should produce not only the print-out of the table as seen on the screen but also, in case the bank manager questions the derivation of the figures, a print-out showing the formulae used in it.

In October, the business finds that it is proceeding very much as had been planned and that advance orders suggest that sales are likely to rise to 150 from January falling to 130 from April. This is extremely encouraging but leaves the business with the problem of how it is going to be able to satisfy the demand.

Production capacity of 120 ovens a month has been sufficient to cope with demand thus far but...

Overtime working, which will inevitably increase labour costs, seems to be called for and the business is to consider how this can be organised. The directors have already talked to staff and sufficient staff have said they would be willing to work overtime.

It is estimated that when production rises above 120 per month each microwave will add £40 to labour costs. Also, while the factory is working overtime, overheads will rise to £5,800 per month. New machinery and maintenance costs of £12,000 will have to be paid for in April.

● Use your existing spreadsheet model as a starting-point, modify accordingly and extend the cash budget to June, investigating some of the possibilities. You may assume that only labour costs and the added overheads will be affected by the overtime working and should remember that selling microwaves that have not been produced is not an acceptable means of improving cash flow.

● So that you have a record of the consequences of the alternative strategies you have investigated, you should print copies of the spreadsheets with sub-headings which indicate what strategy you were examining.

─── 11.13 Council house survey ───

On examination of the sample spreadsheet in **Screen dump 11.13**, it should be self-evident what is required from the survey in terms of the initial data.

The aim is to show in graphical form the types of housing stock that exist within this fictitious borough and the number of people living in the housing.

From the spreadsheet you are to extract a number of bar graphs (or pie charts) showing the distribution of the total housing among the various groups and how the number of occupants are distributed among each accommodation type. You will be able to produce a large number of useful charts from such figures.

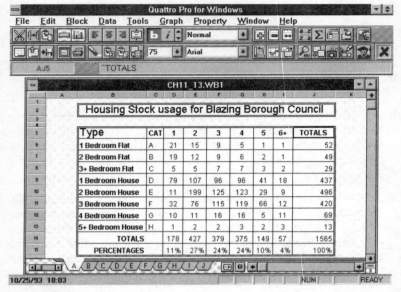

Screen dump 11.13

Produce a number of such charts displaying different aspects of data so that someone else can understand the data quickly and easily without having to read through the table.

When setting up a bar chart or pie chart, one of the problems you will soon face is avoiding too much congestion on the screen.

Name each graph you create as you work through this exercise and present the graphs in the form of a slide show as explained in Chapter 9.

12

———— GLOSSARY ————

Abort. The action of stopping the execution of a program while it is still running. If you are in the middle of updating a record, for example, you may need to abort to avoid a serious error. In Quattro Pro this is usually done by pressing the **Esc** key.

Absolute reference. In a formula, a reference to a cell that does not change when you copy the formula. An absolute reference always refers to the same cell or block. To create an absolute cell reference, enter a $ (dollar sign) before the page reference, column letter, and row number ($January:$C$5) when you write the formula. To create an absolute block name, enter a $ (dollar sign) before the block name ($QUANTITY). For example, if you copy the formula +$A$1*B10 entered in cell C10 to C11 and C12, the formula changes to +$A$1*B11 and $A$1*B12 respectively. The absolute reference ($A$1) does not change.

Access. Referring to data stored in a file. For example, disk access is needed if a Sales Ledger activity is to keep customer records updated.

Algorithm. A series of instructions set up in logical order and designed to perform an activity such as sorting stock records into stock number order. The algorithm will be capable of being converted into a computer program.

Amend. Changing a record in a file. For example, altering a customer's address in a database is a form of file amendment. The term can also be applied to altering the details of a spreadsheet file in order to update a set of figures.

Analyst. A person who has the job of analysing various activities, for example, systems analyst, database analyst, cost analyst. With respect to the system analyst, such people are often concerned with analysing computer-based information systems or manual systems with a view to computerising them. The use of a spreadsheet may be one of many applications an analyst will consider.

Annotating. The process of creating and editing objects such as polygons, text boxes and rectangles. Such annotated objects can be created in a chart and subsequently added to spreadsheets and graphs.

Append. Adding new records to a database table.

Application. A specific use to which a computer is put, e.g. spreadsheet, payroll, accounting, word processing. Such applications are often performed on a computer by a software package, or part of an integrated software package.

Arrow keys (pointer-movement keys). Keys that control the movement of the cell pointer, menu pointer, and insertion point. These keys include UP, DOWN, LEFT, RIGHT, PAGE UP, PAGE DOWN, and HOME, and can be combined with CRTL and END to move around spreadsheets in the same file and other active files.

@ functions. Built-in formulae that will perform specialised calculations automatically. For example, @SUM(block) adds all numbers in the specified block. Quattro Pro has a large number of such functions covering many specialist areas as well as the more general ones.

Background Printing. A process whereby the computer prints a document while continuing to allow an operator to use the computer or computer terminal to process data. One of the benefits of working in a Windows environment is that background printing is now common practice.

Backing Storage. Often referred to as secondary storage, it allows data to be stored on media such as disks for long-term storage purposes, i.e. off-line data storage.

Backup. A process of copying all data from one source to another for safe-keeping. This option is offered by Quattro Pro when you attempt to save a file that already has a file with that name.

Block name. A name assigned to a block of cells or a single cell. To see a list of the block names in the spreadsheet, press function key **F3** (NAME) when writing a formula or specifying a block in an object inspector.

Borders. These are the column letters and row numbers around the notebook area that identify cell locations.

Borland. The name of the company that created the Quattro Pro for Windows package. This company also produces software for other applications.

Buffer. A part of memory used as a temporary store to hold data from an input device. For example, most printers have a buffer memory for storing data prior to printing it. Also, keyboards often hold at least one line of data before it is sent to the computer's processor.

Bug. An error in a program

Bus. A means of communication channel which data travel along. Such channels consist of a control bus, data bus, address bus and peripheral bus.

Button. A small button-like object on the screen that, when clicked on with a mouse, runs a macro.

Byte. A measure of computer memory, normally containing 8 single bits. Each byte often represents a single character. 1024 of these bytes is referred to as a Kilobyte.

Cache Memory. A form of buffer memory that works at high speed and is capable of keeping up with a computer's CPU. It acts as a buffer between the CPU and the slower main memory. Because the CPU is not delayed by memory access, processing is speeded up. The operating system will load segments of programs into cache memory from disks.

Carriage return. A single character sent to the computer by pressing the Return or Enter key on the keyboard. Such carriage returns are often used to release data from the keyboard buffer to the computer's processor.

Cascading windows. Different windows one behind the other. Cascading spreadsheets will give the image of spreadsheets piled up. You will have to have more than one spreadsheet open at any time to get the benefit of this.

Cell. The basic unit of a Quattro Pro spreadsheet. The intersection of a column and a row forms a cell. You enter and store data in a cell.

Central processing unit. Often referred to as the processor or microprocessor and is the main unit of any computer system. The processor accepts its data from input devices, processes the data and sends it to output devices such as screens and printers, or to a disk for saving.

Character. A single element in coded form for the processor, such as a letter or a single number digit. Such characters are normally 8 bits, or one byte, long.

Click. To press the mouse button and quickly release it.

Clipboard. A storage area Windows uses to store data temporarily when you use Edit or Cut. The Clipboard contents are released back on to the spreadsheet using the Paste facility.

Clock. A processor contains an electronic pulse generator that is used to transmit synchronised pulses to different parts of the computer for the interpretation and execution of instructions. The synchronisation is set at a speed that determines the computer's CLOCK SPEED. Such clock speeds are measured in Megahertz (MHz). The faster the clock speed, the faster the internal processing speed of the computer.

Closing files. Closes the current file and moves the cell pointer to the next open file. When you close a file, Quattro Pro removes the file from memory but does not delete the file from disk.

COM. Computer Output on Microfilm. A form of computer output that offers an effective form of long-term data storage that is both compact and durable. Such output is especially useful as a means of archiving data.

Command. An instruction to the computer to perform a given task.

Computer Aided Design (CAD). The use of a computer with graphics software to design through electronic drawing. Main applications areas are in the field of engineering drawing, product design, fashion design and technical drawing.

Control Unit. That part of the computer's Central Processing Unit or micro processor which controls the movements of data within it.

Corruption. A term used to refer to the loss, or corruption, of data. Data corruption is a particular problem when it occurs on a disk. Such corruption can often render data on a disk useless, hence the importance of regular backing up of data.

Creating a chart. A chart is an illustration of data in your worksheet. Charts are effective ways to present data. They can make relationships among numbers easy to see because they turn numbers into shapes (lines, bars, slices of pie), and the shapes can then be compared with one another.

Criteria. A facility that sets out the conditions against which records are extracted or deleted from a database. A criteria table has to be set up on Quattro Pro for this facility to work.

Cursor. A small image such as a block or dash on the screen to indicate where data will be entered from the keyboard.

Customising. A process of altering a package or environment to suit a particular application. You can customise all icons in the Quattro Pro package or create a set of new ones.

Date formats. In Quattro Pro, dates are represented by values from 1 (the date for 1 January 1900) to 73050 (the date number for 31 December 2099). A date number does not look like a date unless you format the cell where it appears. After you format the cell, the date appears in the cell, the date number continues to appear in the input line.

Drag. To press the mouse button and hold it while moving the mouse.

Dedicated computer. A computer system set up to perform one specific task or set of tasks. For example, a cash dispenser or an electronic cash till.

Default. When offering a choice to users through software, a default value is assumed if no choice is made.

Diagnostic routine. A program used to detect errors in either existing software or hardware. Many diagnostic routines will operate in a way that does not interfere with normal operations and is not apparent to a user.

Dialogue boxes. These appear during various procedures and require the user to select options.

Disk Drive. A peripheral device for storing data generated by the computer's processor and for retrieving data by the processor. Disk drives can contain either floppy disks or hard disks.

DOS (Disk Operating System). Part of the software which is loaded into computer memory and is used to operate the computer system.

Drag and drop. A mouse action allowing you to move or copy data around the spreadsheet.

Driver. A part of the Operating System software that is used to control certain peripheral devices.

Edit undo. Reverse the effects of the most recently executed command or action that you can undo.

Electronic Mail. A process of electronically transmitting messages (mail) between computers. Such mail can be stored for future reference.

ERR. A special value that either Quattro Pro generates to indicate an error in a formula or you generate with @ERR. ERR can ripple through formulas: any formula that refers to a cell that contains ERR will itself result in ERR, and any other formula that depends on the formula also results in ERR. When you correct the formula that contains an error, the results of dependent formulas also become correct. The label ERR is not equivalent to the value ERR.

Field. A labelled column in a database or query table that contains the same type of data for each record. For example, an employee database table may contain fields labelled First Name, Last Name, and Employee Number.

File. A collection of records that are related in some way. A stock file, for example, may be a collection of stock records.

File Protection. A method of protecting files from corruption or accidental erasure. A common way of protecting a file is to write protect it, which means files can be read but not written to.

Floppy disk. A backup medium used to store data. Such disks require a disk drive in order for the computer to read from them and write to them.

Flowchart. A diagrammatic way of showing functions and sequences of events within a system or sub-system. Flowcharts can take different forms, such as program flowcharts depicting the way a program runs or systems flowcharts showing the way a system works.

Group Mode. This styles all pages in a spreadsheet in the same manner. When a set of pages, or sheets, is grouped, the alteration of style in any one of them becomes common to all.

Hard Copy. Printed output from a computer.

Hardware. The computer system, including processor and drives.

Help. Help provides information about all aspects of Quattro Pro. To select a Help topic when Quattro Pro is in Ready mode, press function key F1 or click on the Help menu from the menu bar. A list of topics can then be selected by clicking with the mouse. Alternatively, if you are in the middle of a process, such as typing details into an object inspector, then activating Help will give you topics specific to the process.

Housekeeping. A term used to describe the practice of removing unwanted information from disk storage. Good housekeeping speeds up processing and lessens the chance of filling up a disk unnecessarily.

IBM. A trade Name for International Business Machines.

ICL. A trade Name for International Computers Limited.

Icon. Pictorial representation of programs and options available for executing or processing. In Quattro Pro, Icon buttons let mouse users click on commonly used commands and macros. These are fully customisable.

Image Processing. The process of transmitting pictures and images in digitised form.

Input. The process of entering data, either manually or electronically, into a computer.

Installing. The process of implementing software on to a computer for the first time.

Integer. A whole number.

Kilobyte (K). Used to measure data quantity. It represents 1024 bytes of data.

Label-prefix characters. The first character in a label entry defines the label as an entry and controls how Quattro Pro aligns the label in a cell. Quattro Pro does not display the label prefix character in the cell but does display it in the input line when you select a cell that contains a label. Characters: ' (apostrophe) left-aligns (default); " (quotation mark) right-aligns; ^ (caret) centres labels; \ (backslash) repeats one or more characters across the cell.

Landscape Printing. This turns a page sideways on when printing. It is particularly useful when a spreadsheet is wide and occupies only a few rows.

Local Area Network (LAN). A system that connects a number of microcomputers together so that they can share common resources such as a database or printer. While resources can be shared, each computer on a network is still able to act independently of the other.

Logging In. A method of getting access to a computer's information. Designed for security, the process of logging in requires an operator to enter identification and, normally, an associated password.

Logging out. Signing off a system. This should be done whenever an operator has finished work on a computer.

Macro. A stored sequence of commands that automates a task.

Menu. A list of options to choose from. With Quattro Pro the pull-down menus offer the first level, with options from each pull-down menu offering further options.

Merge. Combining two related files.

Mode indicator. An indicator on the spreadsheet that informs the operator about the status of the spreadsheet. For example, READY indicates the spreadsheet is waiting for input while WAIT indicate the computer is busy.

MODEM (Modulator/Demodulator). A device for sending and receiving signals down a telephone line, thereby allowing data communication between computer devices. Such modems will be needed at both ends of a line for data communications to work.

Mouse. An input device that interacts with the screen. It moves the image of an arrow or bar around the screen and is used to select options when a mouse button is clicked.

MS-DOS. A Trade Name for MicroSoft Corporation's Disk Operating System.

Multiplexer. A communications device that receives data from a number of computer devices and then sends such data down ONE telephone line. There will be a slowing down in data communications transmission from each device as more of them transmit data, but such devices can reduce the costs of data communications quite considerably.

Object. An item that can appear in the form of a shape or box on a spreadsheet and be edited, deleted or moved around the spreadsheet. A graph, for example, is a collection of such objects.

Off-Line. A general term referring to data or part of a computer system being inaccessible. If a printer is off-line it will not print.

Operating System. Software that is used to operate the computer and its peripherals.

Operator. A term used to describe a person who operates a computer. This is different from a person who programs a computer, a computer programmer.

Optical Character Reader. A computer input device that recognises characters, usually in typed form. Such devices can be considerable labour saving devices when text that has already been typed needs to be entered to the computer.

Password. A way of ensuring that only authorised personnel have access to parts of a system. Passwords are only effective if they are kept secret from everyone excluding authorised persons. Passwords are also set up in a way that ensures different people have access to different parts of the system.

Paste. The process of pasting what is stored in the clipboard to another part of the spreadsheet, or to a different application altogether.

Peripheral Device. Input, Output, and Storage devices of a computer that constitute part of the system hardware.

Protocol. Communications protocol is a standard of data communications that tries to ensure compatibility in the way data are communicated across lines.

Range. A block of cells referenced by the top left and bottom right cells to give a rectangular block.

Relative reference. In a formula, a reference to a cell or to a block that changes when you copy or move the formula. A relative reference refers to the location of the data in relation to the formula. A relative reference can be an address or block name. For example, if the formula +A1+A2 is in cell A4 and you copy this formula to B4, the formula changes to +B1+B2. A1 and A2 are relative references, which means that they refer to the values entered in cells two and three rows above the formula. After you copy the formula, the relative references still refer to the cells two and three rows above the formula. If you do not want a cell or block address to change when you copy a formula, use an absolute reference.

ROM (Read Only Memory). A part of the memory in a computer used to store programs in a permanent way. Part of a computer's operating system (e.g. BIOS) is stored in ROM. Some systems will also have applications software built into ROM.

Run. The actual execution of a program.

Scheduling. A process of determining the order in which jobs are performed or executed. Such activities can be carried out automatically or by operating, with priorities being set on certain jobs. This tends to be important when working on networked systems.

Scroll box. The square box in a scroll bar, which you drag with the mouse pointer to make another area of the worksheet, dialogue box or object inspector become visible.

Scrolling. A process of running text up the screen when you want to view data beyond the bottom of the screen. Windows uses scroll bars for just this purpose.

Slide show. A facility within the Quattro Pro package of automatically showing a sequence of graphs and annotated objects in a defined sequence for a specific amount of time or a sequence that can be shown by a user controlling it. Such slide shows are of particular benefit for exhibitions and presentations.

Software. All computer programs, from the operating system to applications software.

Sort. A data processing term used when rearranging files into a different order.

Status. A signal indicating whether a system is active or not.

Styles. Enhancements applied to the current selection using the Style commands. Styles include bold, italics, underlining, frames, lines, colour, patterns, alignment, typeface, type size, and number formats.

Suite. A set of inter-related programs. A term often used instead of package.

Tiling windows. The method of displaying a number of screens (windows) at the same time by splitting the screen into sections.

Tutorial. To learn Quattro Pro by completing a series of interactive tutorials, you can choose Interactive Tutors from the Help pull-down menu. The resulting screen lists a wide range of tutorial topics grouped into A Quick Look at Quattro Pro, Understanding Quattro Pro Object, Entering Data, Modifying Notebooks, Printing, and Graphs. Clicking on the Index from this screen allows you to select tutorial help on a specific topic.

Updating. The process of altering a spreadsheet or database.

Visual Display Unit (VDU). The screen that displays text and graphics.

Window. A method of sectioning the screen in such a way that an operator can see different parts of a spreadsheet or, run and see different applications at the same time.

Window Cascade. Sizes open windows. Arranges them one on top of the other, with just the title bars showing.

Word Processing. An application that involves processing words and spending time perfecting format, spelling and so on before producing hard copy.